Great Bread

E·ve·ry Ti·me

65 delectable recipes,
plus simple, proven techniques
for making high-rising breads,
rolls, muffins, and doughs
every time you bake

Marilyn Barbe

St. Martin's Press
New York

With special thanks to...

◎◎

— *My students, past and present, whose enthusiasm, encouragement and good humour have led to the writing of this book.*

— *Gerry, my husband, for his support and for eating those first trials and errors without complaint.*

— *Jeannie Ross for her superb step-by-step recipe illustrations and kind patience.*

— *Perry D'Elia and Company for their creative and organizational input of everything from front to back. They made it such a rewarding experience.*

First published in Canada in 1982 under the title *Basically Bread*.

Library of Congress Cataloging-in-Publication Data

Barbe, Marilyn.
    Great bread every time / Marilyn Barbe.
        p.   cm.
    Includes index.
    ISBN 0-312-07765-3
    1. Bread. I. Title.
TX769.B235   1992
641.8'15—dc20

92-135
CIP

First U.S. Edition: May 1992

10 9 8 7 6 5 4 3 2 1

Revivers of a Lost Art

I call breadmaking at home an art. Now, our grandmothers and great-grandmothers would sit back in their rocking chairs and enjoy a good laugh if we were to tell them that. To these dear ladies, living in a rural setting, and caring for a hungry brood, breadmaking was a necessity that enslaved them to the kitchen.

So, why do I call breadmaking an art? Well, from the earliest French settlements in Canada, where wheat was ground in the seignorial mill and baked in brick ovens, to the turn of this century, Canadian bread was made in the home. Then, as more and more people moved to the city, large bakeries sprang up to fill an ever increasing demand for easy to obtain, cheap bread. And so, our mothers broke an age old tradition, they did not learn how to make bread, and they could not pass the knowledge on to their sons and daughters. So, here we are, enticed by stories of delicious home made bread and a lovely fragrance permeating the house but no one to show us how to make bread. Now we are ready to revive a lost art.

Index

The Secret to Success

Welcome to the world of breadmaking. Now, I'm often asked if making bread is easy and my answer is: "Yes, if you practice," because practice makes perfect, as with everything else. While breadmaking is not a simple process, it is not as time consuming and complex as you want to believe. And, the reward is in the satisfaction you will receive when you serve nutritious homebaked goodies to family and friends.

Whoever said that breadmaking was simple never tried to teach himself or herself how to make bread as I did. You see, the reason why I am writing this cookbook is to help you avoid the mistakes that I made as a novice bread maker. Mistakes? Yes, I'll admit to it, and I think that I made all of them.

I am a self-taught home baker and I know now that had someone taught me the art I would have saved myself a lot of trouble. But, I also know that had someone else taught me I would not be offering you this book.

My initial interest in making home made bread was fuelled by the desire to create bread's wholesome goodness in my own home. Goodness with a gourmet touch. My first results were rock-hard bread-bricks that my wonderful husband ate without complaint. But, that was in the past, and now, after years of baking bread at home and years of teaching the art to hundreds of eager students, I feel that I can offer you a simplified approach to the process. I hope that it will help you avoid all the mistakes that I made.

This approach has one secret to success: that is, read Getting Off to a Good Start before you start. Don't try to make bread without understanding the process - it will never work and you will quit before giving home made bread an honest try. Getting off to a Good Start is a step-by-step explanation of the recipes that follow. Now pour yourself a good cup of tea or coffee, hide away in a secluded spot, and read about bread before you start to make it.

Getting Off To A Good Start

The primary character in this production is yeast. No yeast - no bread - it's as simple as that. All the other ingredients play a secondary role to this fellow, and because he is so important, they cater to his every need. You should too!

Yeast is fussiest about temperature. If your room and the dough ingredients are cold he will take his own good time to grow, and it will take you twice as long to make bread. If your ingredients are too hot you will kill the poor little fellow, and your bread will never rise. The ideal temperature then, is between 80°-100°F (30°-38°C).

Now don't try to get your kitchen that warm. When you read about fool-proof-proofing you will discover how you can cope with a cool kitchen.

Your main concern, before you start, is to remember that the ingredients must all be cozy warm for the benefit of the yeast.

I always use active dry yeast - it's so easy to use! It stores well and keeps up to a year in the refrigerator. The cake yeast works as well as the active dry, but you must use it within a week of purchase. While some people recommend that you freeze yeast I do not because I believe that it damages the yeast cells.

The more yeast you buy, the cheaper it is. If you are in the habit of buying the little foil pouches of yeast, you should know that they are equal to 1 tablespoon of canned yeast, which is much cheaper. Keep opened cans of yeast in the fridge so that the yeast will remain dormant.

Now that you have been introduced to the most important character, read on to learn the essentials of making good bread. You will discover that it is a simple step-by-step process that seldom ever varies, that is why there are procedural headings in the recipes. Once you master the basics the world of bread making is yours.

○○

PROOF THE YEAST

Proofing the yeast means that you want it to start growing. Note that the water temperature should be quite warm to the touch, a little hotter than a baby's bottle. Measure the warm proofing water into a measuring cup, or for larger amounts of water, into a small bowl. Pour the proofing sugar (usually 1 teaspoon) into the water but don't stir; you want the yeast to fall on top of it. While warm water softens yeast, sugar feeds it.

Now that you have the perfect spot for the yeast to start growing, measure the yeast and slowly sprinkle it into the water. Every tiny particle must get wet to soften or it will not start growing. So, if any particles decide to do the backstroke on top of the water, shake the cup gently and they will sink to the bottom. Do not stir the yeast; if you do, it will not be as fluffy.

Place the yeast in a warm spot to proof for 10 minutes. During this time, notice that the particles will expand and pop up to the top of the water. Then, as the yeast grows, it will fill the cup with a thick, foamy, fragrant sponge. If you are not careful it will grow out of the cup and make a mess on the counter. After 10 minutes look at the underside of the cup. If it has a complete layer of dark yeast particles coating it, stir the mixture so that they will also get wet. Wait another minute to soften.

If the yeast has not become foamy after 10 minutes, start over again. This time make sure that the water temperature is correct. If you doubt the quality of the yeast, throw it out and buy a can that is fresh.

MIXING THE INGREDIENTS

During the 10 minute proofing time you should gather the remaining ingredients together. First, melt the butter, margarine or shortening called for in the recipe. Then, the liquids can be poured into the bread bowl along with the sugar, eggs, salt, and any other seasoning that the recipe might call for. Stir until well mixed.

By now your yeast should be ready, so stir it down with a fork and add it to the liquids in the bowl. Then add 1 cup of flour to protect the yeast from the fat. Stir this flour in well and add the **cooled** melted fat or the oil.

ADD THE FLOUR — Getting to dough you

Beginners beware. This is where you usually make a mistake. A recipe always tells you the amount of flour to use. This is just a guide line and not gospel. There are many factors which determine how much flour to use: humidity, growing conditions while the wheat was maturing, room temperature, age of the flour, etc. It all has to do with the flour's absorbancy rate - the more absorbant the flour, the more you will use. But, there is no simple test to tell you the absorbancy rate. So you are your own judge as to how much flour will actually go into the dough. After a little practice you will know by the "feel" of the dough, if it is right. Follow the guideline closely, making sure that you do not add too much flour. If you add too much flour, the dough will be too heavy for the yeast to push up.

So how do you go about making a dough? Well, all that liquid in your bowl, with 1 cup of flour and the fat is a batter not a dough. Now is the time to add the remaining flour to make a dough. Remember to keep the sides of the bowl clean at all times, this gives you a smoother dough.

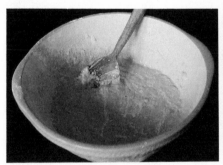

If you are making a two loaf recipe, add the flour 1 cup at a time and give it a good stir in between each addition until you have added the final cup. Don't stir the final cup in. Instead, use it to coat the dough so that you can feel what the consistency is.

Now, ask yourself this question: "Does the recipe call for a soft or a stiff dough, or something in between?" A softer dough goes into loaf pans, muffin tins, etc. A stiff dough goes onto a baking sheet or cookie sheet and has a certain shape that you want it to retain, eg. braiding.

So, to determine the consistency, poke the floured dough with your finger or squeeze it with your hand. Is it floppy and wet (soft) or does it retain it's shape and feel a bit dry (stiff)? If it is too soft, and you want a stiff dough, add another cup of flour and stir it in. If it is stiff, and you want a soft dough, you're too late. But don't worry, it should turn out as long as it is not too stiff.

9

⊙⊙

The easiest way to make bread is to add all of the flour while the dough is still in the bowl. Kneading in an extra cup of flour is difficult unless the dough is very soft. So make sure that it is the proper consistency before going on to the next step. That means, don't be afraid to add an extra cup of flour if you think that the dough is too soft. Also, do not get the terms wet and soft mixed up. The dough at this stage is always wet, that is why you should keep it lightly coated with flour.

KNEAD —
Gluten Power; as the dough said to the baker: "You knead me."

Kneading is the magic of breadmaking. There is a protein in flour and when this protein gets wet, and is agitated, it forms gluten. Gluten can be likened to a bunch of very elastic balloons and, at the first stage of kneading, they have not been made yet. Then, as you knead, the gluten is being made and it traps yeast within it. The yeast, in a warm dough rich with sugar, starts to produce carbon dioxide gas. In time the trapped carbon dioxide will blow up the gluten balloons making the dough rise.

The more you knead the stronger the gluten will be. A good kneading time is 10 minutes for 5 to 10 cups of flour. The beginner should knead for 2-5 minutes longer.

Your kitchen table or a counter top is ideal for kneading. Dust the area where you want to knead with 2 tablespoons of flour. Is the dough in your bowl wet and sticky? If it is, lightly coat it with flour, it will be easier to handle.

Are the sides of your bowl clean and is all the extra flour incorporated into the dough? They should be.

Now, turn your bread bowl on it's side and the dough should fall out onto the floured kneading surface. If it doesn't fall out easily, give it a push with a rubber scraper. Then, flour your hands and gently roll the dough into a ball. You are now ready to knead.

Place the finger tips of both of your hands under the dough opposite you. Now lift and roll the dough towards you so that the dough is half moon shaped. Push the newly exposed surface down with the heel of your hand and give the dough a quarter turn. Continue rolling, pushing, and turning and notice how the texture of the dough changes. A seam will form in the dough, always have it facing upwards. If you do this properly the underside of the dough will stretch, become very smooth and will be easy to work with. Lightly powder this smooth surface, whenever it is too sticky, using only 1 teaspoon of flour.

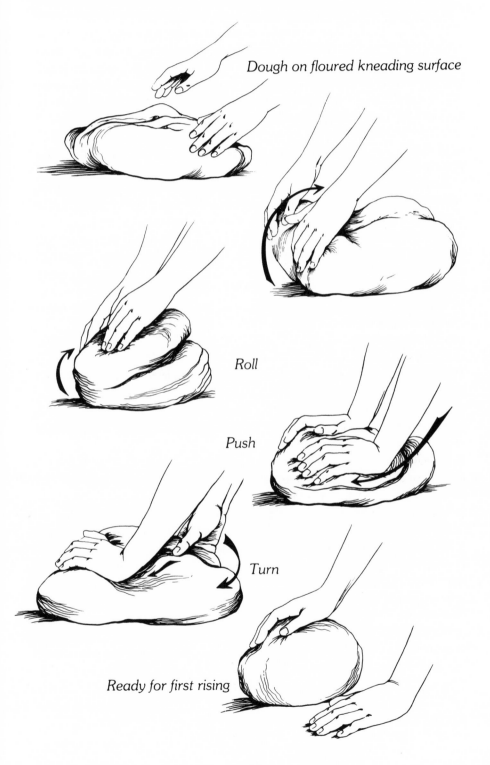

Dough on floured kneading surface

Roll

Push

Turn

Ready for first rising

11

Kneading time is extremely important. Always set a timer to ensure that the dough has been kneaded for 10 minutes or more.

As you knead, you will notice that the dough is undergoing a change. It transforms itself from a sticky, lumpy, slack Mr. Hyde to a smooth, silky, elastic Dr. Jekyll. And, depending on how accomplished a kneader you are, you will notice that this change can be timed in minutes. For the first 5 minutes the dough is harder to manage. Be gentle with it at this stage. If you are too rough, the dough will stick to the kneading surface and to your hands. Every time the dough becomes very sticky give it light powderings, then it will turn easier for you.

If the dough is unmanageable, that is, if it is too wet and slack, and constantly sticks to your hands, then you don't have enough flour in the dough; add another 1/2 cup at once and quickly knead it in.

After 5 minutes, the gluten is becoming well developed and as it develops, the dough is less sticky. Try kneading without flour. You can also be rougher with the dough, but not so rough that it will stick to the kneading surface. The less flour you use at this point the easier it is to determine if the dough has been kneaded sufficiently.

HOW CAN YOU TELL IF THE DOUGH HAS BEEN WELL KNEADED?

Before baking:

1) The dough is smooth and very elastic. It should feel slightly moist to the touch.

2) Bubbles have formed over the entire surface of the dough, and it "pops" as you knead it. This means that the gluten has trapped the yeast which is giving off carbon dioxide gas.

After baking:

1) The bread has a lovely, fine texture. It is not coarse and crumbly.

2) It has a fresh taste, not too yeasty.

The important point to remember is that kneading takes 10 minutes, or more - use a timer. Beginners, always knead for more than 10 minutes until you get into the rhythm. It is difficult to determine when whole wheat doughs have been kneaded sufficiently so keep a special eye on the timing.

GREASING THE BOWL

Wash and dry the bread bowl. Coat the inside of the bowl with margarine, butter, shortening or lard. Do not use oil because it is so thin that it is readily absorbed into the dough, and does not prevent sticking. Pick the dough up and don't worry if it has stuck to the counter, that's natural, just scrape it off with a spatula. Place the dough, smooth side down, into the bowl and turn it over so that now the top is greased. This coating of grease prevents the top from drying out.

FOOL-PROOF-PROOFING — The first round

Summer is the best time to make bread - your kitchen is usually so warm! But what do you do during long winters when the kitchen seems to be the coldest room in the house? The solution is as near as your oven. That's right, your oven is the perfect "proofing box." Professional bakers have large rooms (proofing boxes), which are kept warm and humid, where their dough will be placed to proof, that is, for the first and second risings. The home baker doesn't need anything so elaborate - just an oven.

Fool-proof-proofing is basically the same procedure for first and second risings, only the times vary. So, for the first rising, boil 2 cups of water in a saucepan. Place the saucepan on the bottom rack of your oven, then put your **uncovered** bread bowl on the rack directly over top of the water. If your oven has a light in it, then turn it on; if there is no light, reheat the water half way through the rising time. The hot water and lightbulb are a perfect source of heat and humidity to encourage the growth of yeast. Do not turn your oven element on, it will make the oven too hot for long proofing. Fool-proof-proofing normally takes $1\frac{1}{2}$ hours for the first rising and 30-45 minutes for the second rising.

○○○

There will be times, of course, when your oven is otherwise occupied. In that case, it should also be giving off enough heat to help the bread rise, so put the bread bowl close to your stove. If you put the bowl on the stove be careful, it's usually too hot and the dough will start to cook - most unpleasant. Whenever your dough rises on a counter top or near the stove, cover it with a tea towel to keep it free from drafts. Never cover dough with a wet cloth, you'll be surprised when you discover that 1/3 of the dough is stubbornly clinging to the towel as you try to remove it. Plastic wrap is another cover to avoid. If you use it, especially for the last rising, the surface of the dough will not be smooth, but rough and pitted.

PUNCH DOWN AND SHAPING — The knock out punch

After the 1½ hours of the first rising the dough should be double in bulk. Remember the size of the dough before it started to rise, is it double that now? Poke 2 of your fingers into the top of the dough and wiggle them. Do your fingers move freely, do the dents stay in when you remove your fingers? If so the dough is ready for shaping, if not, let the dough rise for 15 minutes more. Occasionally the dough will collapse when you poke it; this means that the dough has risen more than double. No problem here.

Now quickly punch the center of the dough down with your fist. Pull the dough away from the sides of the bowl, towards the center. Pick the dough up out of the bowl and place it on a counter top. Don't use any flour, the grease already on the dough should stop it from sticking. But, if the dough is unmanageable lightly oil your hands with cooking oil. Now knead the dough for a minute or two to break the large bubbles.

During this first rising the gluten and yeast have matured, but the yeast is still not evenly distributed, therefore, it requires a second rising.

Letting the DOUGH REST — the end of round one:

You will notice that every time you handle the dough it stiffens up: handling tightens the gluten. Therefore, shaping the dough into a desired form is difficult immediately after punching down and kneading. At this point the dough always wants to spring back instead of doing what you want it to do. So, the only thing you can do is to let it rest from 5 to 10 minutes so that it loosens up.

(For whole wheat and other "sticky doughs" see page 18).

Cut the dough into the number of loaves that you are making (usually 2). Shape them into smooth balls and let them rest, uncovered, on the counter top. After 5 to 10 minutes a dry skin will form on the smooth top of the dough while the underside will stay moist.

After the dough has relaxed you will be ready to shape a sandwich loaf, or any of the other shapes that are described in this book.

⊙⊙⊙

SHAPING A SANDWICH LOAF

The sandwich loaf is the most common shape in North American breadmaking. The dough can be softer for this loaf because the pan supports the sides as the dough rises. If it is too soft though, it will flop over the sides of the pan instead of rising out of it.

To shape the loaf turn one of the smooth dough balls over so that the dried surface is on the bottom. Flatten the stickier part with your hands (don't use flour or oil) so that the dough is a rectangle that is 3 times the width of your loaf pan and as wide as the pan is long.

Don't make it too long and wide or it will wrinkle when you try to get it into the loaf pan. Flip the dough over to make sure that the dry side is smooth, if not, smooth it out with your hands, then flip it over again. If the dough has been well rested no force should be required, you should simply be patting the dough. The rougher you are the more the dough will tear and stick.

Tightly roll the dough towards you. As you do keep sealing the seam with your thumbs. When you come to the end pinch the bottom seam shut. Push both ends of the dough in and pinch them shut. Place the dough in a loaf pan, seam side down. If the seam is not directly at the bottom of the pan the dough can unravel during baking. Push the dough up against one side of the pan. While you are doing this make sure that the dough is even throughout, one end should not be fatter than the other because it will bake that way. This step also rounds the top, so don't be tempted to pat the dough down or it will be a "square" loaf.

Now the dough is ready for the second rising. If you are going to do this in the oven remember to reheat the water. Also, don't cover it with a tea towel if it is going into the oven, towels only keep the dough free from draft. An important point to remember is that the newly shaped dough should fill the pan three-quarters full. Make sure that the dough size fits the pan. Too much dough will flop over the sides of the pan and too small an amount of dough will never rise up like you expect it too. (See Sandwich Loaves, page 126).

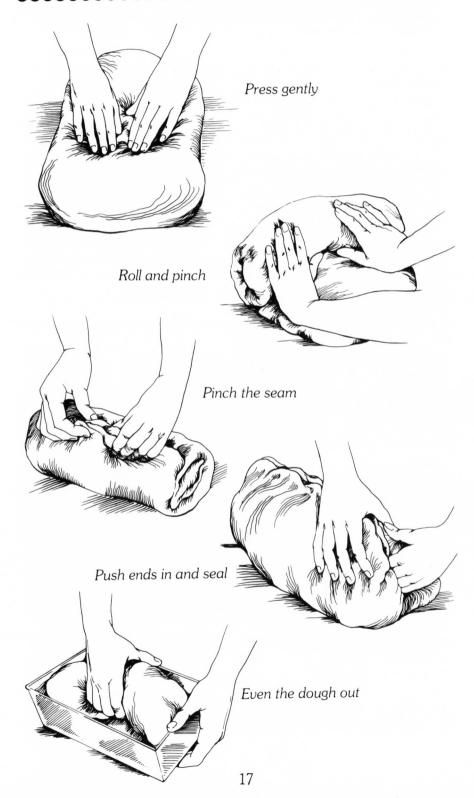

Press gently

Roll and pinch

Pinch the seam

Push ends in and seal

Even the dough out

⦿⦿

SHAPING "STICKY" LOAVES

Some loaves cannot stand the handling that most breads can. Take whole wheat or potato bread for example. They are so sticky that patting them out on the counter will make them stick and your loaf will never be smooth, let alone come off the counter!

Because sticky doughs are not stiff they do not need to rest. After the first rising, knead the dough until you have a smooth surface on the bottom. Flip the dough over and cut in half. Turn one half cut side up, pinch the cut together to smooth the dough out. Place the dough, seam side down in a loaf pan and let it rise a second time the same as you would any other bread.

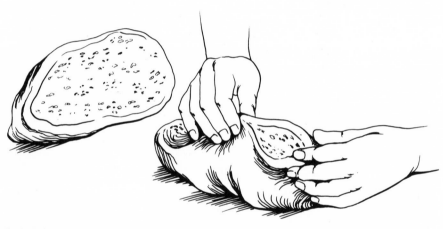

OTHER SHAPES:

The shapes that bread will take are only limited to your imagination. Simply remember the basic rule: a soft dough must go into a pan that will support its sides, and a stiff dough can be free form, that is, you can place it onto a cookie sheet and it will keep its shape.

BRAIDING:

The most important point to remember about braiding is that you must not use flour at any time. Flour makes the braids so slippery that they will not roll. Also, make sure that you are rolling the dough completely over and not just wiggling it around.

Braiding with 3 dough ropes is easy and attractive. Before you start be certain that the dough has rested and has lost its elasticity. Using both hands, roll the dough out into the specified length. If the dough puts up a fight set it aside for a minute to relax, next time you work with it it should be easier to roll.

Now, place the ropes next to each other on a counter, making sure that they are not too close. Pinch the ropes together at one end. Cross 1 rope over its neighbouring rope. Place the remaining rope into the middle of this cross. You will now notice that there is 1 rope that is free, or uncrossed, on the outside; bring it into the middle and keep doing this until the dough is all used up. Pinch the ends together, pick the braid up and place it on a greased baking sheet tucking the pinched ends underneath.

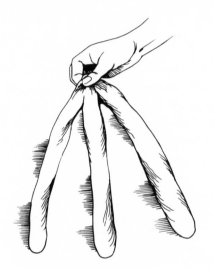

Pinch ends together

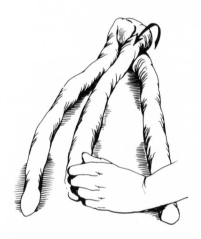

Cross over its neighbour

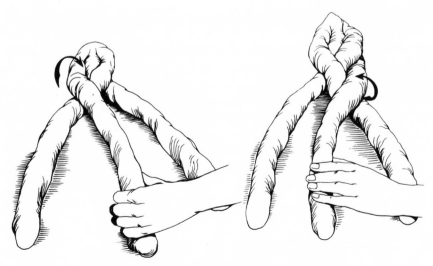

Outside rope goes into the middle

⦿⦿

ROUND LOAVES

Round loaves are easy to make, simply smooth the dough out by kneading a few times. Flip the dough over and you will have a smooth, round, loaf. Place the loaf on a greased cookie sheet, or, for a change, sprinkle the sheet with cornmeal to prevent the dough from sticking. NOTE: Only sprinkle cornmeal where the dough will be placed, otherwise the cornmeal will burn.

When the loaves double gently slash the tops diagonally 3 times with a very sharp or serrated knife. Slashing the top of the loaf prevents the sides from splitting.

FRENCH LOAVES

The secret to these loaves is that the gluten be well relaxed before shaping. If the dough is stiff let it rest for 10 minutes after punching down before attempting to shape it, stretch it into an oblong, then roll the dough into a short, fat, rope, tapering the ends. Place it on a greased baking sheet, seam side down. After rising slash the sticks diagonally 3 or 4 times.

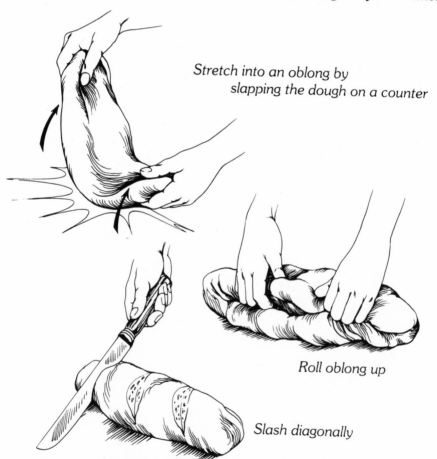

Stretch into an oblong by slapping the dough on a counter

Roll oblong up

Slash diagonally

20

BEFORE BAKING

How can you tell if the dough is ready to bake? Sandwich loaves should be from a 1/2" to an 1" above the pan and the corners of the pan should be filled. For whole wheat breads, the loaves must not double (see page 125 for the reason why), but should just reach the top and fill the corners of the pan. If any bread over rises it will fall during baking.

Special care must be taken with this risen dough; rough handling will make it fall. If the dough does fall or if it has over risen, just turn it out of the pan and reshape it. The third rising is even faster than the second.

Remove the dough from the oven before preheating if you used the fool-proof-proofing method.

Free form loaves are double when they have risen for about 30 minutes in a warm place. If they start to spread out sideways then they are starting to over rise. You can tell if the bread has under risen only after baking. Then there will large splits in the loaves.

GLAZES — The finishing touch

There will be times that a recipe will call for glazing and, if it is not a sugar glaze, now is the time to do it. Glazes are normally brushed on breads made without milk, or on fancier breads such as coffee cakes.

1) MILK GLAZE: Gently brush the dough with milk before baking and once during baking. It darkens the crust giving it a slight gloss.

2) EGG WASH: This is made with 1 egg and 2 tablespoons of milk well beaten together. Make sure that you gently spread the wash on every part of the dough but, don't let it run onto the baking pan where it will burn, and make bread stick to the baking sheet.

3) MELTED BUTTER OR MARGARINE: This glaze softens the crust and can be brushed on either before or after baking. While this initially makes the crust glossy it will dull again once the fat soaks in.

BAKING — the next best thing to eating

When the dough has doubled in size, the oven has preheated, and the glaze has been brushed on, you are ready to bake. Carefully place the pans in the middle of the oven and bake for the time indicated in the recipe. Check the bread now and then to make sure that it is not browning too quickly. Then, should the bread be darkening too soon, loosely cover it with aluminum foil; this will stop the top from burning.

After the bread has baked remove it immediately from the pan. Turn the bread over and tap it on the bottom, does it sound hollow? If the answer is yes then it is done. Another good indication that the bread has finished baking is if it comes out of the pan easily. Usually, bread that sticks to the pan is not cooked yet. But, the best test for doneness is a cake tester. This is a long thin piece of wire usually used for making sure that a cake has been cooked through. Insert the tester into the bottom of the loaf then pull it out, if it is still dry then the bread is baked. Bake the bread for another 5 to 10 minutes if it isn't quite ready.

⊙⊙

Always cool the bread on a cake cooling rack. When you do this the steam escapes from the bread without leaving any soggy areas.

Notice that at the time a loaf of bread first comes out of the oven the top is always hard, then, as the steam escapes, it will soften. You can brush melted margarine, butter or shortening on the crust before it cools if you did not do so before the bread went into the oven.

ICING SUGAR GLAZE — the piece de resistance

Note: Make this just before you use it or it will dry out.

  1 **cup sifted icing sugar**
  ¼ **tsp. almond or vanilla**
     flavouring
  2-3 **tbsp. milk**

Pour the icing sugar and flavouring into a small bowl or measuring cup. Add the milk, 1 tablespoon at a time, stirring well with a fork. The icing should fall in a slow, thick stream when you lift the fork out of the bowl or cup. Now you are ready to glaze. If the icing is too thin add more sugar, if it is too thick add a drop more milk.

Fancy sweet breads like hot cross buns and coffee cakes, that have been egg washed, look even more inviting when they have been drizzled with Icing Sugar Glaze. When this glaze has been spread on a hot loaf just out of the oven it will melt and coat the top with a thin opaque, layer of icing.

For another effect the glaze can be drizzled on the bread with a fork when the bread has **cooled** thoroughly. The icing looks like pretty lacework because it retains its threadlike shape.

You can decorate these fancy loaves with walnut, pecan or almond halves, or even coconut. Glacé cherries are also a very attractive addition, especially during the holiday season. Try decorating with coloured sugar or candied sprinkles, or royal icing flowers and decorations. Just remember to either stick them on immediately after the icing has been applied or use some of the leftover glaze as "glue."

STORAGE

It's important to let all of the steam escape before storing bread; this takes 2 hours. So, after the bread has cooled completely it can be stored in a cupboard or in a freezer. Frozen bread can be kept for up to 6 weeks, after that it will get bitter tasting freezer burn. Don't store bread in the refrigerator because it stales very quickly due to dry air circulating in it.

For the average loaf of bread, the best method of storage is a plastic bag. If the bread was made properly it will stay fresh for 3 days in a plastic bag, but homemade bread doesn't stay around that long in the average household. Crusty breads should be stored in either a bread box or a paper bag, plastic will soften the crust. Fancy breads store, and freeze well in plastic but be careful not to crush the icing.

○○

SLICING BREAD

For those who enjoy their bread hot out of the oven, use an electric knife to slice it. If you don't have an electric knife make pan buns or some other type of bun that will pull apart; hot bread is impossible to slice with a knife.

A good bread knife is a very important tool for those who make their daily bread. Serrated knives catch the bread as they slice and are therefore superior to a straight edged knife. For best results, turn the bread on it's side to slice - you'll find that the slices are of a more even thickness.

Timetable

Length of time	Process	Comments
10 minutes	PROOF yeast	
	Gather ingredients together	
	Mix ingredients	
	Add the flour	
10-12 minutes	KNEAD	
2 minutes	Grease bowl	
	Set bread to proof	
1½ hours	1ST RISING	
	(using fool-proof-proofing)	Take a break
10-12 minutes	Punch dough down	
	Let it rest	
	SHAPE it into loaves	
	Place in/on greased pans	
30-45 minutes	2ND RISING	
	(using fool-proof-proofing)	
	Preheat oven	Take a break
1 minute	GLAZE	
30 minutes	BAKE	Take a break
TOTAL - 2½ hours		2 hour break

Basic Bread Formula

For some strange reason you'll find a bread recipe in your cookbook collection that will not work; the reason being that the author did not follow basic bread chemistry. For example, if a recipe calls for 3 cups liquid and 7 cups flour, the dough will be too slack and will not retain its shape because it has too much liquid. There are thousands of bread recipes but they should correspond with the following "bread equation." So remember, if the recipe that you are using calls for more or less liquid than the equation, it should also call for more or less flour than the equation.

½ **cup warm water for proofing**	*softens yeast*
1 **tsp. sugar**	*feeds yeast*
1½ **tbsp. yeast**	*makes dough rise*
2 **tsp. salt**	*controls growth of yeast*
1 **tbsp. to**	
1 **cup sugar**	*to taste*
2 **cups liquid**	*binding agent*
¼ **cup fat**	*preservative, taste*
7 **cups flour**	*main ingredient, gluten*

Problems??

⦾⦿⦾⦿⦾⦿⦾⦿⦾⦿⦾⦿⦾⦿⦾⦿⦾⦿⦾⦿⦾⦿⦾⦿⦾⦿⦾⦿⦾⦿⦾⦿⦾⦿⦾⦿

Bread won't rise: too much flour in dough, dough too cold, yeast was killed by excessive heat, improper kneading, oven temperature too high, too much salt.

Bread flops over the sides of the pan: bread over risen, too much dough for pan size, not enough salt.

Pale crust: not enough sugar.

Crust uneven and wrinkled: improper shaping.

Bread does not keep well: not kneaded long enough, stored in the refrigerator.

Bread falls during baking: the dough was handled too roughly when placed in the oven, bread over risen (see oven spring page 125).

Egg braid dough is too sticky to work with: this happens when the eggs are not fresh, will usually occur with supermarket eggs.

Bread crumbles when sliced: over risen dough makes a coarse grained dough which crumbles, not enough salt.

Thick crust: oven temperature was too low, bread over baked.

Bread has a strong yeast taste and crumbly texture: not kneaded long enough - (see gluten, page 124).

Dough and bread have a strong alcoholic smell: dough rose in place that was too hot, over risen.

Free-form loaves spread out instead of rise - braids lose their shape: dough too soft.

Rye bread spreads instead of rises: use more white flour.

Dough looks flat after second rising: if you are using tea towels to cover the bread, use only one layer because the dough cannot push up more weight than that.

Make sure that you use the correct pan size for the amount of dough that you are making - (see Sandwich Loaves, page 126).

No oven spring (page 125): oven temperature was too hot.

Sides did not brown like the top crust: new, shiny, aluminum pans, use pre-seasoned pans.

EVERYDAY BREAD

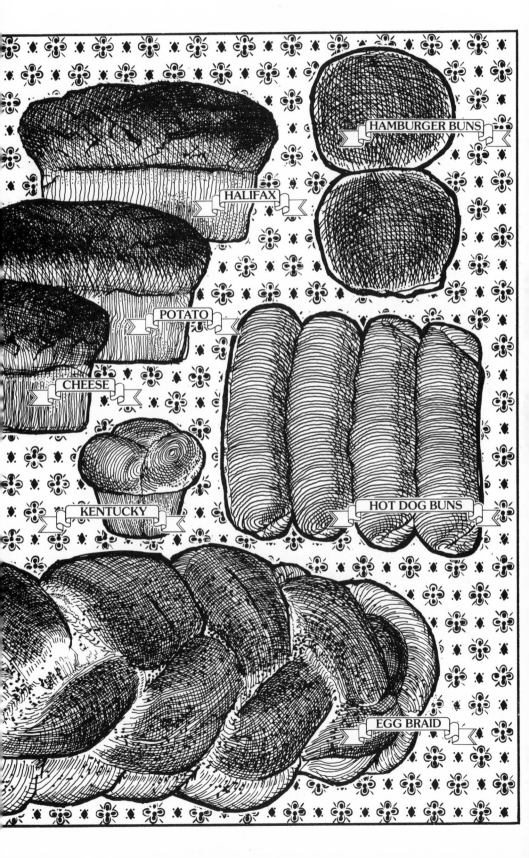

HAMBURGER BUNS

HALIFAX

POTATO

CHEESE

KENTUCKY

HOT DOG BUNS

EGG BRAID

Dave's White Bread

Makes 2- 8"x4"x3" sandwich loaves.

- ½ **cup warm water**
- 1 **tsp. sugar**
- 1½ **tbsp. yeast**
- 2 **cups milk, scalded**
- 2½ **tsp. salt**
- 2 **tbsp. sugar**
- ¼ **cup melted shortening, cooled**
- 7 **cups flour**

PROOF
In a 1 cup measure, pour 1/2 cup warm water. Add 1 teaspoon sugar, but do not stir. Slowly sprinkle 1½ tablespoons yeast into the water, making sure each particle gets wet. Again, do not stir. Wait 10 minutes until the yeast is thick and foamy.

MIX
Meanwhile, pour 2 cups milk into your bread bowl. Add 2 tablespoons sugar and 2½ teaspoons salt and stir. Stir down the proofed yeast with a fork and pour it into the milk mixture. Then stir in 1 cup of flour. Add 1/4 cup of fat, stir.

ADD FLOUR (slowly)
Add remaining flour, 1 cup at a time, until the dough feels rather soft when you poke it with a floured finger.

KNEAD
Make sure the dough is well covered with flour, turn the dough out onto a lightly floured surface and gently knead until it is smooth and elastic: 10 minutes.

1ST RISING
Place the dough into a greased bowl, turn to grease the top, set in a warm, draft-free spot and allow to rise until double: 1½ to 2 hours.

SHAPE
Then punch the dough down, turn out onto a bread board, knead briefly, divide in half. Shape into a smooth ball and allow it to rest for 5-10 minutes, depending on elasticity. Shape each half into loaves (page 16).

2ND RISING
Place into bread pans, set in a warm, draft-free spot and allow to rise until double: 30 to 45 minutes.

BAKE
Bake in a **400°F** oven for **25-30 minutes.** Cool immediately on a wire rack.

Making bread is faster when you use skim milk powder to make the milk - you don't need to scald it.

Halifax County White

The perfect white!

Makes 2- 9"x5"x3" sandwich loaves.

- 1 **cup warm water**
- 2 **tsp. sugar**
- 2 **tbsp. yeast**
- 6 **tbsp. sugar**
- 2 **cups milk, scalded**
- 4 **tsp. salt**
- ¼ **cup melted shortening**
- 9-10 **cups flour**

PROOF
In a 2 cup measure, pour 1 cup warm water. Add 2 teaspoons sugar, but do not stir. Slowly sprinkle 2 tablespoons yeast into the water, making sure each particle gets wet. Again, do not stir. Wait 10 minutes until the yeast is thick and foamy.

MIX
While you are waiting mix the following ingredients in your bread bowl, stirring well between each addition: 2 cups milk, 6 tablespoons sugar, 4 teaspoons salt, the yeast, 1 cup flour and 1/4 cup cooled, melted shortening.

ADD FLOUR (slowly)
Add remaining flour 1 cup at a time and stir well between each addition. Coat the dough lightly with flour before turning it out.

KNEAD
Turn the dough out onto a lightly floured surface and knead for 10 minutes, until smooth and elastic.

1ST RISING
Place the dough in a greased bowl, turn to grease the top, set in a warm, draft-free spot and allow to rise until double: 1½ hours.

SHAPE
When the dough has doubled punch it down and turn it out onto a clean surface. Knead briefly to remove the large air bubbles. Cut the dough in half and let it rest for 5 minutes. Shape into 2 sandwich loaves (page 16). Place in loaf pans.

2ND RISING
Set in a warm, draft-free spot to rise until double: 30-45 minutes.

BAKE
For a glossy crust brush the loaves evenly with milk just before baking. Bake in a **400°F** oven for **30 minutes**. Cool immediately on wire racks.

Potato Bread (*The Consistent Champion*)

○◉○

Makes 2- 8" x 4" x 3" sandwich loaves.

2½	cups warm water (divided)
1	tsp. sugar
1	tbsp. yeast
1½	tbsp. salt
1	tbsp. oil
1	cup mashed potatoes
7-8	cups flour

PROOF

In a bread bowl, pour 1 cup warm water. Add 1 teaspoon sugar, but do not stir. Slowly sprinkle 1 tablespoon yeast into the water, making sure each particle gets wet. Again, do not stir. Wait 10 minutes until the yeast is thick and foamy.

MIX

After 10 minutes add the following, stirring well between each addition: 1 cup mashed potatoes, 1½ cups warm water, 1½ tablespoons salt (yes, that's tablespoons!) and 2 cups flour. Then add 1 tablespoon oil.

ADD FLOUR (slowly)

Add the remaining flour, 1 cup at a time, until you use up most of the 8 cups of flour. This dough will be too sticky to handle if you do not get enough flour into it at this time.

KNEAD

Turn the dough out onto a floured kneading surface and knead until smooth and elastic: 10-12 minutes. Keep the kneading surface lightly dusted with flour if the dough is too sticky to handle.

1ST RISING

When the dough is smooth and elastic, place it into a greased bowl, turn it to grease the top, set in a warm, draft-free spot, and allow it to rise until double in bulk: 1½ hours.

SHAPE

When doubled punch the dough down, pull it away from the sides of the bowl and turn it out onto a lightly floured kneading surface. Knead the dough to remove the large air bubbles: 1 minute. Cut it in half and set it aside to rest for 5-10 minutes.

2ND RISING

Shape the dough into loaves, (page 16), set in a warm, draft-free spot and allow to rise until double: 30 minutes.

BAKE

Bake in a **400°F** oven for **35 minutes**. Cool immediately on a wire rack.

French Canadian Crusty White

High rising free-form loaves, just like our colonial ancestors made.

Makes 2 free-form loaves.

- 2 **cups warm water**
- 2 **tbsp. sugar**
- 2 **tbsp. yeast**
- 1 **tbsp. salt**
- ¼ **cup melted shortening**
- 6 **cups flour**
- **cornmeal**
- **pickling salt (optional)**

PROOF
In a bread bowl, pour 2 cups warm water. Add 2 tablespoons sugar, but do not stir. Slowly sprinkle 2 tablespoons yeast into the water, making sure each particle gets wet. Again, do not stir. Wait 10 minutes until the yeast is thick and foamy.

MIX
After 10 minutes add the following ingredients to your bread bowl, stirring well between each addition: 1 tablespoon salt, 2 cups flour, 1/4 cup cooled, melted shortening.

ADD FLOUR (quickly)
Add remaining flour 2 cups at a time to make a stiff dough. Lightly coat the dough with flour before turning it out.

KNEAD
Turn the dough out onto a lightly floured surface and knead until smooth and elastic: 10 minutes.

1ST RISING
Place the dough in a greased bowl, turn to grease the top, set in a warm, draft-free spot until double: 1½ hours.

SHAPE
When the dough has doubled, punch it down and turn it out onto a clean surface. Knead the dough briefly to break the large air bubbles. Cut the dough in half and shape each half into a smooth round ball. Pour cornmeal on an ungreased cookie sheet, only where the dough will be placed. Place the loaves on the cornmeal.

2ND RISING
Set the loaves in a warm, draft-free spot, allow to rise until double: 30 minutes.

BAKE
Before baking, slash the tops 2-3 times with a very sharp knife. Sprinkle the tops with pickling salt. Bake in a **400°F** oven for **30 minutes.** Cool immediately after baking on a wire rack.

31

Egg Braid

Makes 2 braids.

½ **cup warm water**
1 **tsp. sugar**
2 **tbsp. yeast**
2 **cups warm water**
2 **tsp. salt**

¼ **cup sugar**
2 **eggs**
3 **tbsp. oil**
7 **cups flour**
   sesame or poppy seeds

PROOF

In a 1 cup measure, pour 1/2 cup warm water. Add 1 teaspoon sugar, but do not stir. Slowly sprinkle 2 tablespoons yeast into the water, making sure each particle gets wet. Again, do not stir. Wait 10 minutes until the yeast is thick and foamy.

MIX

While you are waiting for the yeast to proof combine the following ingredients in your bread bowl stirring well between each addition: 2 cups warm water, 2 teaspoons salt, 1/4 cup sugar and 2 eggs. Then stir in the yeast and 2 cups of flour. Add 3 tablespoons oil and stir.

ADD FLOUR (quickly)

This dough should be rather stiff so the braids will retain their shape. Add remaining flour, 2 cups at a time, and stir to make a stiff dough. Coat the dough lightly with flour and turn it out onto a floured kneading surface.

KNEAD

Knead the dough until it is smooth and elastic: 10 minutes. Lightly dust the kneading surface if the dough becomes too sticky to handle.

1ST RISING

Place the dough into a bowl, turn to grease the top, set in a warm, draft-free spot and allow to rise until double: 1-1½ hours.

SHAPE

When the dough has doubled, punch it down, pull it away from the sides of the bowl and turn it out onto the kneading surface. Knead it briefly to break all of the large bubbles. Cut the dough in half and set it aside to rest.

Then cut 1/3 of the dough off of one of the pieces and set it aside. Cut the remaining 2/3 into 3. Roll each piece into a rope 18 inches long. Braid the ropes and place them on a greased baking sheet. Cut the remaining 1/3 dough into 3 small pieces. Roll each out into a rope 16 inches long. Braid these ropes and place them securely on top of the braid already on the baking sheet. Do the same with the second half of the dough.

2ND RISING

Allow to rise until double in a warm, draft-free spot: 30 minutes.

EGG WASH

Brush the braids with egg wash (page 21). Sprinkle with sesame or poppy seeds.

BAKE

Bake in a **400°F** oven for **30 minutes.** Cool on a wire rack.

Oatmeal Bread

OOOOOOOOOOOOOOOOOOOOOOOOOOOOOOOOOOOOOOOOOO

Oatmeal gives the dough a "soggy" feeling. Be careful because it will be easy to add too much flour.

Makes 2- 8"x4"x3" sandwich loaves.

$\frac{1}{2}$ **cup warm water**	$\frac{1}{4}$ **cup molasses**
1 **tsp. sugar**	2 **tbsp. sugar**
2 **tbsp. yeast**	2 **tsp. salt**
3 **cups quick cooking oats**	$\frac{1}{2}$ **cup cold water**
$2\frac{1}{2}$ **cups boiling water**	3 **tbsp. melted margarine**
	6-$6\frac{1}{2}$ **cups flour**

PROOF

In a 1 cup measure, pour 1/2 cup warm water. Add 1 teaspoon sugar, but do not stir. Slowly sprinkle 2 tablespoons yeast into the water, making sure each particle gets wet. Again, do not stir. Wait 10 minutes until the yeast is thick and foamy.

MIX

While you are waiting add the following ingredients to your bread bowl, stirring well between each addition: 3 cups oats, $2\frac{1}{2}$ cups boiling water, 1/4 cup table molasses, 2 tablespoons sugar, and 2 teaspoons salt. Just before you add the yeast cool the mixture with 1/2 cup cold water. Add the yeast, 1 cup flour and 3 tablespoons melted margarine.

ADD FLOUR (slowly)

Add remaining flour 1 cup at a time to make a moderate dough. Coat the dough with flour before turning it out.

KNEAD

Turn the dough out onto a floured surface and knead for 12 minutes until elastic.

1ST RISING

Place the dough in a greased bowl, turn to grease the top, place in a warm, draft-free spot until double: $1\frac{1}{2}$-2 hours.

SHAPE

When the dough has doubled punch it down and turn it out onto a clean surface. Shape into a sandwich loaf as you would for a sticky dough (page 18). Place in 2 greased loaf pans that have been sprinkled with quick cooking oats. If you want, sprinkle the top of the loaves with oats too.

2ND RISING

Place the pans in a warm, draft-free spot, allow to rise until just under double: 30 minutes. **Note:** The dough structure is weak so it will fall in the oven if it over rises.

BAKE

Bake at **400°F** in oven for **30 minutes**. Cool immediately after baking on a wire rack.

Cheese Bread

⊙⊙

Makes 2 braided sandwich loaves (8"x4"x3").

½ cup warm water	1 egg
1 tsp. sugar	2 cups old cheddar cheese,
2 tbsp. yeast	grated
1½ cups milk (scalded)	¼ cup parmesan cheese
¼ cup sugar	¼ cup melted shortening
2 tsp. salt	6 cups flour

PROOF

In a 1 cup measure, pour 1/2 cup warm water. Add 1 teaspoon sugar, but do not stir. Slowly sprinkle 2 tablespoons yeast into the water, making sure each particle gets wet. Again, do not stir. Wait 10 minutes until the yeast is thick and foamy.

MIX

While you are waiting add the following ingredients to your bread bowl, stirring well between each addition: 1½ cups milk, 1/4 cup sugar, 2 teaspoons salt and 1 egg. Then add the proofed yeast, 1 cup flour, 2 cups grated cheese, 1/4 cup parmesan cheese, and 1/4 cup melted shortening. Stir well.

ADD FLOUR (slowly)

Add remaining flour 1 cup at a time to make a soft dough. Make sure that the dough is lightly coated with flour before turning it out.

KNEAD

Turn the dough out onto a lightly floured surface and knead until smooth and elastic: 10-12 minutes.

1ST RISING

Place the dough in a greased bowl, turn to grease the top, allow to rise until double in a warm, draft-free spot: 1½-2 hours.

SHAPE

Turn the dough out onto a clean surface and cut it in half. Cut each half into 3 and roll each piece into a short rope. Braid (page 18) 3 pieces together for each loaf. Tuck each braid into a greased loaf pan.

2ND RISING

Place in a draft-free spot, allow to rise until double: 30-45 minutes.

BAKE

Bake in a **400°F** oven for **30 minutes**. Cool immediately on a wire rack. Brush with butter while still hot.

Note: Add 1 teaspoon of oregano, basil or rosemary to the dough for a herb bread. Add it at the same time as you add the cheese.

Always preheat the oven before baking bread.

Fantastic Cheese Bread

⊙○◎○⊙

Makes 2- 8" x 4" x 3" sandwich loaves.

1 **cup warm water**
1 **tsp. sugar**
1½ **tbsp. yeast**
1 **cup flat beer**
2 **tsp. salt**
¼ **cup sugar**
2 **eggs**
⅓ **cup skim milk powder**

1 **cup old cheddar cheese, grated**
¼ **cup melted shortening**
1 **cup old cheddar cheese, cut into ½-inch cubes and frozen**
6½-7 **cups flour**

PROOF

In a 2 cup measure, pour 1 cup warm water. Add 1 teaspoon sugar, but do not stir. Slowly sprinkle 1½ tablespoons yeast into the water, making sure each particle gets wet. Again, do not stir. Wait 10 minutes until the yeast is thick and foamy.

MIX

While you are waiting for the yeast to proof add the following ingredients to your bread bowl, stirring well between each addition: 1 cup flat beer, 2 teaspoons salt, 1/4 cup sugar, 2 eggs, 1/3 cup skim milk powder, 1 cup grated, old cheddar cheese. Then add the yeast and 1 cup of flour, stir. Add 1/4 cup cooled, melted shortening.

ADD FLOUR (slowly)

Add the remaining flour, 1 cup at a time, to make a moderately soft dough. Make sure that the dough is lightly covered with flour before proceeding.

KNEAD

Turn the dough out onto a very lightly floured surface and knead for 10 minutes. Sprinkle 1 teaspoon of flour on the bottom of the dough whenever it becomes too sticky to work with. Knead until smooth and elastic.

1ST RISE

Place the dough in a greased bowl, turn to grease the top, cover and allow to rise until double: 1½ hours.

Punch the dough down and turn it out onto a clean kneading surface. Knead the frozen cheese chunks into the dough, then cut the dough in half. Shape each half into a smooth ball and allow to rest for 10 minutes.

SHAPE

When the dough is easy to work with, shape it into a sandwich loaf (page 16). Place into 2 greased pans.

2ND RISE

Cover the dough and allow to rise until double: 30 minutes.

BAKE

Bake in a **400°F** oven for **30 minutes**. Cool on wire racks.

Note: Place a cookie sheet under the loaves while they bake to catch any escaped cheese.

Potato-Cheese Bread

⊙⊙

Makes 2- 8"x4"x3" sandwich loaves or 2- 8" round cake tins.

½ **cup warm water**	1½ **cups old cheddar cheese,**
1 **tsp. sugar**	**grated**
1 **tbsp. yeast**	1 **cup mashed potatoes**
2 **cups milk, scalded**	¼ **cup melted shortening**
1 **tbsp. salt**	7-8 **cups flour**
1 **egg**	

PROOF

In a 1 cup measure, pour 1/2 cup warm water. Add 1 teaspoon sugar, but do not stir. Slowly sprinkle 1 tablespoon yeast into the water, making sure each particle gets wet. Again, do not stir. Wait 10 minutes until the yeast is thick and foamy.

MIX

While you are waiting add the following ingredients into a bread bowl, stirring well after each addition: 2 cups milk, 1 tablespoon salt, 1 egg, 1½ cups cheese, 1 cup mashed potatoes, the yeast, 1 cup flour and 1/4 cup melted shortening, cooled.

ADD FLOUR (slowly)

Add remaining flour 1 cup at a time to make a moderately soft dough. Before turning the dough out to be kneaded, make sure that it is lightly coated with flour.

KNEAD

Turn the dough out onto a lightly floured surface and knead until smooth and elastic: 10-12 minutes.

1ST RISING

Place the dough in a greased bowl, turn to grease the top, set in a warm, draft-free spot until double: 1½ hours.

SHAPE

Punch the dough down, turn it out onto a clean surface and knead briefly to remove the large bubbles. Cut the dough in half and proceed as you would with a sandwich loaf (page 16). Or, for a party, place in round cake tins.

2ND RISING

Place in a warm, draft-free spot and allow to rise until double: 30 minutes.

BAKE

Bake at **400°F** in oven for **30 minutes.** Cool immediately after baking on a wire rack.

Make the milk with skim milk powder: it's cheap and you don't need to scald it.

nice bread — not too much onion taste

Onion Buns or Bread

⊙○⊙○⊙○⊙○⊙○⊙○⊙○⊙○⊙○⊙○⊙○⊙○⊙○⊙○⊙○⊙○⊙○⊙

Makes 18 buns or 2- 8" x 4" x 3" sandwich loaves.

2 **cups warm water**	¼ **cup melted shortening**
1 **tsp. sugar**	8 **cups flour**
2 **tbsp. yeast**	1 **cup onions, finely**
2 **eggs**	**chopped**
1 **tbsp. salt**	2 **tbsp. butter**
½ **cup sugar**	**poppy seeds**

PROOF
In a bread bowl, pour 2 cups warm water. Add 1 teaspoon sugar, but do not stir. Slowly sprinkle 2 tablespoons yeast into the water, making sure each particle gets wet. Again, do not stir. Wait 10 minutes until the yeast is thick and foamy.

MIX
While you are waiting, sauté the onions in butter until they start to brown. Set aside to cool. Then add the following to your bread bowl, stirring well between each addition: 2 eggs, 1 tablespoon salt, 1/2 cup sugar, 1 cup flour, 1/4 cup cooled, melted shortening, 1 cup sautéed onions.

ADD FLOUR (slowly)
Add remaining flour 1 cup at a time to make a moderately soft dough. Make sure that the dough has a light coating of flour before turning it out.

KNEAD
Turn the dough out onto a lightly floured surface and knead until smooth and elastic: 10-12 minutes.

1ST RISING
Place the dough in a greased bowl, turn to grease the top, allow to rise until double in a warm, draft-free place: 1½ hours.

SHAPE
Cut into 18 pieces to make hamburger bun shapes (page 42).
Cut into 24 pieces to make dinner rolls (page 38).
Cut into 2 pieces for sandwich loaves (page 16). If you want to make round loaves, use 8 inch pie plates so that the sides have some support.

2ND RISING
Place in a warm, draft-free place until double in bulk: 30 minutes.

EGG WASH
Brush with egg wash (page 21) just before baking and sprinkle with poppy seeds.

BAKE
Buns: **400°F** oven for **10-15 minutes,** until golden brown.
Bread: **400°F** oven for **30 minutes**.

Exposed raisins, candied fruit, currants and cheese will burn during baking. Pull them off before baking.

Dinner Rolls

◉◉

I call these rolls "clouds" because they are so light, they are a perfect addition to any meal.

Makes - See SHAPE section.

2 **tbsp. yeast**	½ **cup sugar**
½ **cup warm water**	3 **eggs**
1 **tsp. sugar**	½ **cup melted shortening**
½ **cup milk, scalded**	5 **cups flour**
2 **tsp. salt**	

PROOF

In a 1 cup measure, pour 1/2 cup warm water. Add 1 teaspoon sugar, but do not stir. Slowly sprinkle 2 tablespoons yeast into the water, making sure each particle gets wet. Again, do not stir. Wait 10 minutes until the yeast is thick and foamy.

MIX

Meanwhile, add the following ingredients to your bread bowl, stirring well between each addition: 1/2 cup cooled milk, 2 teaspoons salt, 1/2 cup sugar, 3 eggs, the proofed yeast, 1 cup flour, 1/2 cup cooled, melted shortening.

ADD FLOUR (slowly)

Add remaining flour 1 cup at a time to retain a soft dough. Coat the dough lightly with flour before turning it out.

KNEAD

Turn the dough out onto a lightly floured surface and knead until smooth and elastic: 10-12 minutes. If the dough becomes sticky, lightly powder the bottom with flour.

1ST RISING

Place the dough in a greased bowl, turn to grease the top, place in a warm, draft-free spot to rise until doubled: 1½ hours.

SHAPE

When the dough has doubled turn it out onto a clean surface and knead for 2 minutes to release the large bubbles. The number of buns you will make depends on the size of your muffin tins, the usual number is 18 but could be more or less depending on the size of the tin. So, roll the dough into an 18 inch long rope and cut it into 18 pieces. To make cloverleaf rolls cut each piece into 3, roll each piece into a smooth ball and place the 3 pieces into a greased muffin tin. The dough should fill the muffin tin 3/4 full. You can also cut each of the 18 pieces in half to make a roll that will easily split in 2, or leave each piece whole, shape it into a ball and place it in a muffin tin, that's the fastest way of doing it.

Dinner Rolls (continued)

⊙⊙⊙⊙⊙⊙⊙⊙⊙⊙⊙⊙⊙⊙⊙⊙⊙⊙⊙⊙⊙⊙⊙⊙⊙⊙⊙⊙⊙⊙⊙⊙⊙⊙⊙⊙

2ND RISING
Set the muffin tins in a warm, draft-free spot and allow to rise until double: 30 minutes.

BAKE
Bake in oven at **375°F** for **15 minutes**. Remove from tins immediately after baking, brush with melted butter. Serve warm.

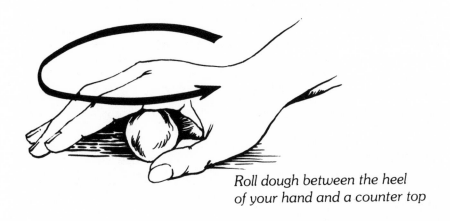

Roll dough between the heel of your hand and a counter top

A Big Batch of White

⊙⊙

This recipe is a big undertaking. Make sure that you have the basics conquered before trying it. This is a great way to make the week's bread all at once.

Makes 6- 8"x4"x3" sandwich loaves.

8 **cups warm water**	2 **tbsp. salt**
½ **cup sugar**	1 **cup skim milk powder**
2½ **tbsp. yeast**	½ **cup melted shortening**
2 **eggs**	22-24 **cups flour**

PROOF

In a bread bowl, pour 8 cups warm water. Add 1/2 cup sugar, but do not stir. Slowly sprinkle 2½ tablespoons yeast into the water, making sure each particle gets wet. Again, do not stir. Wait 10 minutes until the yeast is thick and foamy.

MIX

Add the following ingredients stirring well between each addition: 2 eggs, 2 tablespoons salt, 1 cup skim milk powder, 4 cups flour, 1/2 cup cooled shortening.

ADD FLOUR (quickly)

Add remaining flour 3 cups at a time to get a moderatley soft dough. Make sure that you have a strong wooden spoon for this recipe. Coat the dough well with flour before turning it out.

KNEAD

Turn the dough out onto a lightly floured surface and knead until smooth and elastic: 15-20 minutes.

1ST RISING

Place the dough in a greased bowl, turn to grease the top, set in a warm, draft-free spot until double: 2 hours.

SHAPE

Punch the dough down, turn it out and knead it for 2 minutes. Cut the dough into 6 pieces and shape each into a smooth ball. Allow the dough to rest for 10 minutes then shape into sandwich loaves (page 16). Place in greased loaf pans.

2ND RISING

Set the loaf pans in a warm, draft-free spot and allow to rise until doubled: 30-45 minutes.

BAKE

Bake in a **400°F** oven for **30 minutes.** If your oven does not heat evenly switch the loaves around so that they will brown evenly. Cool immediately after baking on wire racks.

For whole wheat fans see "A Big Batch of Whole Wheat" page 57.

Old Kentucky Home Rolls

⊙⊙

An unusual potato recipe that's big enough to feed the whole gang. Serve one-half freshly baked and freeze the other half to warm up later.

Makes approx. 3 dozen.

1	**cup water**
1	**tsp. sugar**
2	**tbsp. yeast**
3	**cups milk, scalded**
1	**cup sugar**
1	**cup shortening**
1½	**tbsp. salt**
1	**cup mashed potatoes**
1	**tsp. baking soda**
2	**tsp. baking powder**
10-12	**cups flour**

PROOF
In a 2 cup measure, pour 1 cup warm water. Add 1 teaspoon sugar, but do not stir. Slowly sprinkle 2 tablespoons yeast into the water, making sure each particle gets wet. Again, do not stir. Wait 10 minutes until the yeast is thick and foamy.

MIX
While you are waiting for the yeast to proof, cream 1 cup sugar and 1 cup shortening until light and fluffy. Mix in 1 cup mashed potatoes and beat well. Then add 3 cups milk, 1½ tablespoons salt and 4 cups flour. Add the proofed yeast and stir well.

1ST RISING
Set the bowl to rise in a warm place for 1½ hours. Add 2 teaspoons baking powder and 1 teaspoon baking soda, then:

ADD FLOUR (slowly)
Add remaining flour 1 cup at a time to make a soft dough. Lightly coat the dough with flour before turning it out.

KNEAD
Turn the dough out onto a lightly floured surface and knead until smooth and elastic. Let it rest for 10 minutes before shaping.

SHAPE
See page 38 for shaping instructions.

2ND RISING
Set in a warm, draft-free spot and allow to rise until double: 20-30 minutes.

BAKE
Bake in a **400°F** oven for **10-15 minutes.** Cool on a wire rack immediately after baking. Brush with melted margarine or butter if desired.

Hotdog and Hamburger Buns

◎◎◎

Makes 8 hamburger and 10 hotdog buns.

2 **cups warm water**
1 **tsp. sugar**
2 **tbsp. yeast**
½ **cup sugar**
3 **eggs**
1 **tbsp. salt**
¾ **cup melted shortening**
8 **cups flour**

PROOF

In a bread bowl, pour 2 cups warm water. Add 1 teaspoon sugar, but do not stir. Slowly sprinkle 2 tablespoons yeast into the water, making sure each particle gets wet. Again, do not stir. Wait 10 minutes until the yeast is thick and foamy.

MIX

Then add 1/2 cup sugar, 3 eggs, 1 tablespoon salt, and 1 cup flour. Stir well until the mixture is smooth. Mix in 3/4 cup cooled, melted margarine.

ADD FLOUR (slowly)

Add remaining flour 1 cup at a time to make a moderately soft dough. Make sure that the dough is lightly coated with flour before turning it out.

KNEAD

Turn the dough out onto a lightly floured surface and knead until smooth and elastic: 10-12 minutes.

1ST RISING

Place the dough in a greased bowl, turn to grease the top, place in a warm, draft-free place. Allow to rise until double: 1½ hours.

SHAPE

You can make hotdog and hamburger buns at the same time or use the dough for only one type of bun. So, cut the dough in half and use 1/2 for:
Hamburger buns - cut half into 8 pieces and shape into smooth balls. Place balls on a greased cookie sheet and flatten slightly.
Hotdog buns - cut the other half into 10 pieces and shape into smooth balls. Let them rest. Then, using a rolling pin, flatten each ball into an oblong 6"x2". Roll it up lengthwise and place it seamside down on a greased baking sheet. Place them in rows so that they will touch as they rise, then they will remain straight.

Hotdog and Hamburger Buns

⦿⦿

2ND RISING

Place shaped buns in a warm, draft-free place, allow to rise until double 20-30 minutes.

BAKE

Bake in a **375°F** oven for **20-25 minutes**. Cool immediately on a wire rack.

Note: Before baking you can brush the buns with egg wash (page 21) and sprinkle with poppy or sesame seeds.

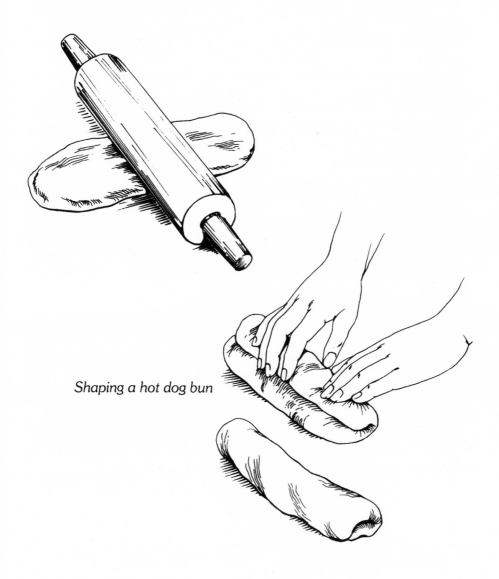

Shaping a hot dog bun

Rye Bread

Makes 2 free-form loaves.

2½ **cups warm water**
2 **tbsp. yeast**
¼ **cup sugar**
1 **tbsp. salt**
2 **tbsp. oil**
2½ **cups rye flour**
4½-5 **cups white flour**
1-2 **tbsp. caraway seeds**

PROOF

In a bread bowl, pour 2½ cups warm water. Add 1/4 cup sugar, but do not stir. Slowly sprinkle 2 tablespoons yeast into the water, making sure each particle gets wet. Again, do not stir. Wait 10 minutes until the yeast is thick and foamy.

MIX

Stir in 1 tablespoon salt, 2½ cups rye flour, 2 tablespoons oil and 1-2 tablespoons caraway seeds.

ADD FLOUR (slowly)

Add the flour, 1 cup at a time, until it is incorporated into the dough. This dough tends to be rather stiff.

KNEAD

Knead for 15 minutes, until the dough is very smooth.

1ST RISING

Place in a greased bowl, turn to grease the top, set in a warm, draft-free spot and allow to rise until double in bulk: 2 hours.

SHAPE

When double, punch the dough down and knead very briefly. Large bubbles rarely form in the dough. Shape into either a round loaf (page 20) or a french stick (page 20). Sprinkle baking sheet with cornmeal only where the bread will be placed, otherwise the cornmeal will burn.

2ND RISING

Place dough over cornmeal, set in a warm, draft-free spot and allow to rise until double: 30 minutes.

BAKE

Slash the loaves before baking. Bake in **400°F** oven for **30 minutes**. Cool on a wire rack.

44

Sourdough Rye

⊙⊙⊙⊙⊙⊙⊙⊙⊙⊙⊙⊙⊙⊙⊙⊙⊙⊙⊙⊙⊙⊙⊙⊙⊙⊙⊙⊙⊙⊙⊙⊙⊙⊙⊙⊙⊙

Makes 2 free-form loaves.

> STARTER:
> 1 **tbsp. yeast**
> 1¼ **cups warm water**
> 1 **tsp. sugar**
> 1 **tbsp. cider vinegar**
> 1¼ **cups flour**

PROOF

In a bread bowl, mix 1 tablespoon yeast, 1¼ cups warm water, 1 teaspoon sugar, 1 tablespoon cider vinegar and 1¼ cups flour. Stir well, cover with a tea towel and let stand overnight in a warm place. The next day the sourdough should have a sour smell and should appear quite spongy.

> 2 **cups warm water**
> 1 **tbsp. salt**
> 1 **tbsp. oil**
> 6 **cups rye flour**
>
> 2 **cups white flour**
> **cornmeal**
> **caraway seeds, optional**

MIX

Add 2 cups warm water, 1 tablespoon salt, 1 tablespoon oil and 6 cups rye flour to sourdough mixture.

ADD FLOUR (slowly)

Add 2 cups white flour to get a stiff dough.

KNEAD

Turn dough out onto a floured surface and knead until smooth: 12 minutes. At this point the dough should feel very stiff, after the first rising it will feel lighter.

1ST RISING

Place dough in a greased bowl, turn to grease the top, place in a warm, draft-free spot and allow to rise until double in bulk: 2 hours.

SHAPE

When dough has doubled turn it out and shape into either french sticks (page 20) or round loaves (page 20). Don't knead unless large bubbles appear on the surface.

Sprinkle cornmeal on a greased cookie sheet only in those places where the dough will sit. Place dough on the cornmeal.

2ND RISING

Set in a warm, draft-free spot and allow to rise until double: 45 minutes.

BAKE

Slash the tops diagonally with a sharp knife two or three times. Bake in a **400°F** oven for **30 minutes**. Cool immediately on a wire rack.

WHOLE GRAIN BREAD

WHOLE WHEAT DINNER ROLLS

PROTEIN BREAD

RED RIVER BREAD

A BIG BATCH OF WHOLE WHEAT

CARMELITE BREAD

Whole Wheat Wisdoms

Two types of flour are derived from the wheat kernel. If the wheat is winter wheat, it produces soft wheat flour that is low in protein and therefore low in gluten; it is not recommended for making bread. Spring wheat produces hard wheat flour, and with it's higher protein content it is ideal for making bread. Non-wheat flours are low in the gluten-forming protein and must be combined with wheat flour for the dough to rise.

Whole wheat flour is made from the milling of the entire wheat kernel. Whereas white flour is composed of only the starchy endosperm, whole wheat flour has the added goodness of the bran and germ.

Wheat germ has a high fat content and will therefore become rancid if stored for too long. As a result, you cannot keep whole wheat flour for as long as pure white flour.

Bran, in breadmaking, weakens the gluten during first and second rising so you should not let the dough rise for as long as white flour breads. Whole wheat breads will fall during baking if they have over risen. The rule to follow is that the dough should rise until just under double.

100% and 60% whole wheat breads do not rise as high as white flour breads. Watch that they do not over rise.

Bread dough made with whole wheat flour may feel elastic but will never feel smooth after kneading because of the bran and germ. Guarantee that your kneading time is 10 minutes or the dough will not rise as expected.

Hands vs. Machine

The only equipment you require to make good bread is a large bowl, a wooden spoon, an apron and your hands. Now, this is a cookbook about the basic breadmaking method, and what could be more basic than kneading with your hands? I recommend that you learn this basic method first, and then go on to machines if you wish. Each machine, whether it is a food processor, blender, or heavy duty mixer, comes with it's own set of instructions. Use these instructions to adapt the recipes in this book to your machine.

"The Quickie"

In a hurry? Try this recipe, it's quick and good. Breads made with a large percentage of whole wheat flour do not have the same texture as white flour breads, therefore you can get away with eliminating some of the steps you would normally use.

Makes 2- 8" x 4" x 3" sandwich loaves.

- 2¼ **cups warm water**
- 1 **tsp. sugar**
- 1½ **tbsp. yeast**
- ¼ **cup blackstrap molasses,**
  or honey
- ¼ **cup melted shortening**
- 4 **cups whole wheat flour**
- 2 **cups white flour**
- 2 **tsp. salt**

PROOF
In a bread bowl, pour 2¼ cups warm water. Add 1 teaspoon sugar, but do not stir. Slowly sprinkle 1½ tablespoons yeast into the water, making sure each particle gets wet. Again, do not stir. Wait 10 minutes until the yeast is thick and foamy.

MIX
Then add the following ingredients to the yeast, stirring well between each addition: 2 teaspoons salt, 1/4 cup molasses, 1 cup whole wheat flour, and 1/4 cup cooled shortening.

ADD FLOUR (slowly)
Add 3 cups whole wheat flour and 2 cups white flour, 1 cup at a time and stir well to make a moderately soft dough. Coat the dough lightly with white flour before turning it out.

KNEAD
Turn the dough out onto a lightly floured surface and knead until elastic: 10 minutes. Shape the dough into a ball and let it rest for 10 minutes.

SHAPE
Cut the dough in half and shape as you would sticky loaves (page 18). Place in greased pans.

ONLY RISING
Place the loaf pans in a warm, draft-free spot and allow to rise until double: 30-45 minutes.

BAKE
Bake in oven at **400°F** for **30 minutes**. Cool immediately on a wire rack.

Healthy Whole Wheat

○◉○

Makes 2- 8" x 4" x 3" sandwich loaves.

1¼ **cup warm water**
1 **tsp. sugar**
2 **tbsp. yeast**
1 **cup milk, scalded**
1 **egg**
2 **tsp. salt**
3 **tbsp. sugar**
¼ **cup bran**
¼ **cup wheat germ**
¼ **cup rolled oats**
¼ **cup sesame seeds**
2 **cups whole wheat flour**
2 **tbsp. oil**
3 **cups white flour**

PROOF

In a 2 cup measure, pour 1¼ cups warm water. Add 1 teaspoon sugar, but do not stir. Slowly sprinkle 2 tablespoons yeast into the water, making sure each particle gets wet. Again, do not stir. Wait 10 minutes until the yeast is thick and foamy.

MIX

Combine the following ingredients in your bread bowl, stirring well between each addition: 1 cup milk, 1 egg, 2 teaspoons salt, 3 tablespoons sugar, 1/4 cup bran, 1/4 cup wheat germ, 1/4 cup rolled oats, 1/4 cup sesame seeds. Stir the yeast down with a fork and add it to the mixture in your bread bowl. Then, stir in 2 cups whole wheat flour and 2 tablespoons oil. At this stage the mixture should look like porridge.

1ST RISING

This process is called a sponge. Set the bread bowl aside and allow the mixture to become foamy: 1 hour.

ADD FLOUR

Stir the mixture down and add 2½-3 cups of white flour, 1 cup at a time, stirring well between each addition. Then turn the dough out onto a floured kneading surface.

KNEAD

Knead until elastic: 10-12 minutes.

SHAPE

Cut the dough in half and quickly shape it into loaves (page 18). Place the loaves into greased loaf pans.

2ND RISING

Set in a warm, draft-free spot, allow to double: 30 minutes.

BAKE

Bake in a **400°F** oven for **30 minutes.** Cool immediately on a wire rack.

Whole Wheat Bran Bread

These loaves are smaller than the usual, small and delicious.

Makes: 2- 8" x 4" x 3" sandwich loaves.

½ **cup water**
1 **tsp. sugar**
1 **tbsp. yeast**
2 **tsp. salt**
1 **cup milk, scalded**
2 **tbsp. sugar**

2 **eggs**
2 **tbsp. molasses**
6 **tbsp. melted margarine**
2 **cups whole wheat flour**
2 **cups bran**
2 **cups white flour**

PROOF
In a 1 cup measure, pour 1/2 cup warm water. Add 1 teaspoon sugar, but do not stir. Slowly sprinkle 1 tablespoon yeast into the water, making sure each particle gets wet. Again, do not stir. Wait 10 minutes until the yeast is thick and foamy.

MIX
Mix the following ingredients in your bread bowl, stirring after each addition: 2 teaspoons salt, 1 cup cooled milk, 2 tablespoons sugar, 2 eggs, 2 tablespoons molasses, the yeast, 1 cup whole wheat flour, 2 cups bran and 6 tablespoons cooled margarine.

ADD FLOUR
Add 1 cup whole wheat flour and 2 cups white flour. Coat the dough with white flour before turning it out.

KNEAD
Turn the dough out onto a lightly floured surface and knead until elastic: 10 minutes.

1ST RISING
Place the dough in a greased bowl, turn to grease the top, set in a warm, draft-free spot until double: 1½ hours.

SHAPE
Punch the dough down, turn it out onto a clean surface and knead it for 1 minute to release the large bubbles. Cut the dough in half and shape each half into a smooth ball. Wait 5 minutes for the dough to relax. Shape as you would a sandwich loaf (page 16). Place in greased pans.

2ND RISING
Set the pans in a warm, draft-free spot, allow to rise until double: 30 minutes.

BAKE
Bake in oven at **400°F** for **30 minutes.** Cool immediately on a wire rack.

Tim's Health Bread

Makes 2- 8" x 4" x 3" sandwich loaves.

- 2 **cups warm water**
- 1 **tbsp. honey**
- 2 **tbsp. yeast**
- 1 **cup milk, scalded**
- 1 **tbsp. salt**
- ¼ **cup soy flour**
- ¼ **cup cracked wheat**
- ½ **cup barley flour**
- 1 **cup graham flour**
- 3 **tbsp. oil**
- 3 **tbsp. blackstrap molasses**
- 2 **cups wholewheat flour**
- 3-4 **cups white flour**

PROOF

In a bread bowl, pour 2 cups warm water. Add 1 tablespoon honey, but do not stir. Slowly sprinkle 2 tablespoons yeast into the water, making sure each particle gets wet. Again, do not stir. Wait 10 minutes until the yeast is thick and foamy.

MIX

Then stir in 1 cup of cooled milk, 1 tablespoon salt, 1/4 cup soy flour, 1/4 cup cracked wheat, 1/2 cup barley flour, 1 cup graham flour, 3 tablespoons oil and 3 tablespoons molasses. Stir well.

ADD FLOUR (slowly)

Add 2 cups whole wheat flour, 1 cup at a time, then add the white flour, 1 cup at a time. Lightly coat the dough with flour.

KNEAD

Turn the dough onto a lightly floured kneading surface and gently knead for 10 minutes.

1ST RISING

Place in a greased bowl, turn to grease the top, set in a warm, draft-free spot and allow to rise until double: 1½ hours.

SHAPE

Punch dough down, turn out, knead briefly. Cut dough in half, shape into loaves (page 18) and place in greased loaf pans. Set in a warm, draft-free spot and allow to rise until double: 30 minutes.

BAKE

Bake in **400°F** oven for **35-40 minutes**. Cool immediately on a wire rack.

Protein Bread

◎◎

Makes 2- 8"x4"x3" loaves.

- ½ **cup honey**
- 2½ **cups water**
- 2 **tbsp. yeast**
- 2 **cups whole wheat flour**
- ⅓ **cup oil**
- 1½ **cups rye flour**
- ½ **cup rolled oats**
- ½ **cup soy flour**
- ½ **cup wheat germ**
- ½ **cup bran**
- ¾ **cup skim milk powder**
- 1 **tbsp. salt**
- 3-4 **cups white flour**

PROOF
In a bread bowl, pour 2½ cups warm water. Add 1/2 cup honey, but do not stir. Slowly sprinkle 2 tablespoons yeast into the water, making sure each particle gets wet. Again, do not stir. Wait 10 minutes until the yeast is thick and foamy.

MIX
While you are waiting for the yeast to proof, combine 2 cups whole wheat flour, 1½ cups rye flour, 1/2 cup rolled oats, 1/2 cup soy flour, 1/2 cup wheat germ, 1/2 cup bran, 3/4 cup skim milk powder and 1 tablespoon salt in another bowl and stir. Add 1 cup of this dry mixture to proofed yeast then stir in 1/3 cup oil. Add the rest of the dry mixture, 1 cup at a time and stir well after each addition.

ADD FLOUR (slowly)
Start adding 3-4 cups white flour 1 cup at a time to make a moderate dough.

KNEAD
Turn dough out onto a lightly floured surface and knead gently for 10 minutes.

1ST RISING
Place in greased bowl, turn to grease the top and set in a warm, draft-free spot and allow to rise until double: 1½ hours.

SHAPE
Punch dough down, turn out and knead briefly. Divide in half, shape into loaves (page 18) and place in greased loaf pans.

2ND RISING
Set in a warm, draft-free spot and allow to rise until double: 30 minutes.

BAKE
Bake in a **400°F** oven for **35-40 minutes**. Cool immediately on a wire rack.

Red River Bread

⊙⊙

Makes 2- 8" x 4" x 3" sandwich loaves.

 2½ **cups warm water**
 1 **tsp. sugar**
 1½ **tbsp. yeast**
 ¼ **cup honey**
 2 **tsp. salt**
 1 **cup Red River cereal**
 ¼ **cup melted shortening**
 2 **cups triticale flour**
 3½ **cups white flour**

PROOF
In a bread bowl, pour 2½ cups warm water. Add 1 teaspoon sugar, but do not stir. Slowly sprinkle 1½ tablespoons yeast into the water, making sure each particle gets wet. Again, do not stir. Wait 10 minutes until the yeast is thick and foamy.

MIX
Add the following ingredients, stirring well between each addition: 1/4 cup honey, 2 teaspoons salt, 1 cup Red River cereal, 2 cups triticale flour, 1/4 cup melted, cooled shortening.

ADD FLOUR (slowly)
Add flour 1 cup at a time to incorporate all 3½ cups of flour. Coat dough with flour before turning out.

KNEAD
Knead on a lightly floured surface for 10-12 minutes, until elastic and not as sticky as it was at first.

1ST RISING
Place the dough in a greased bowl, turn to grease the top, and allow to rise until double in a draft-free spot: 1½ hours.

SHAPE
Shape into sandwich loaves (page 18) and place into 2 greased loaf pans.

2ND RISING
Place in a warm, draft-free spot for 30 minutes, until almost doubled.

BAKE
Bake in oven at **400°F** for **30 minutes.** Cool on wire racks immediately after baking.

Triticale flour is milled from a newly developed grain which is a combination of rye and wheat. It is available in health food stores.

Gloria's Raisin Oatmeal Bread

⊙⊙⊙

Makes 2- 8" x 4" x 3" sandwich loaves.

- ¼ **cup warm water**
- 1 **tsp. sugar**
- 2 **tbsp. yeast**
- 2 **cups boiling water**
- 1 **cup quick cooking oats**
- 3 **tsp. salt**
- ¼ **cup margarine**
- ½ **cup honey**
- ½ **cup finely chopped walnuts**
- 1 **cup raisins**
- 3 **cups whole wheat flour**
- 2 **cups white flour**

PROOF
In a 1 cup measure, pour 1/4 cup warm water. Add 1 teaspoon sugar, but do not stir. Slowly sprinkle 2 tablespoons yeast into the water, making sure each particle gets wet. Again, do not stir. Wait 10 minutes until the yeast is thick and foamy.

MIX
In bread bowl, combine 2 cups boiling water, 1 cup oats, 3 tsp. salt, 1/4 cup margarine, 1/2 cup honey, and 3 cups whole wheat flour - 1 cup at a time. Stir to cool, then add proofed yeast. Add 1 cup raisins, 1/2 cup walnuts, and 1 cup white flour. Stir well. Dough may seem stiff. If moist, coat mixture with 1/2 cup flour (reserve remaining half to dust kneading surface and for kneading).

KNEAD
Turn dough out onto lightly dusted kneading surface and gently knead for 10 minutes. Dough may feel sticky, this is due to the combination of whole wheat flour, honey, and margarine, be careful not to add too much flour.

1ST RISING
Place dough in a greased bowl, turn to grease the top, set in a warm, draft-free spot and allow to rise until double: 1½ hours.

SHAPE
Punch dough down, turn onto kneading surface, and knead briefly. Cut in half, shape into loaves (page 18), and place in greased loaf pans.

2ND RISING
Set in a warm, draft-free spot and allow to rise until double: 30 minutes.

BAKE
Bake in a **400°F** oven for **40 minutes**. You may want to lower the heat to 350°F during the last 10 minutes of baking. Cool immediately on a wire rack.

Whole Wheat Dinner Rolls

⊙⊙⊙

Although it may seem like a good idea to serve 100% whole wheat rolls for dinner, there are a few points to ponder before you go ahead with your plans. Remember 100% whole wheat products are more filling. If you are planning a large meal your guests won't have enough room to try all the other delectables you've prepared. A good rule to follow is that a dinner roll should complement, not dominate a meal. Here's a recipe that fits the bill:

Makes 16-20 rolls

> 1 **tbsp. yeast**
> 1 **cup warm water**
> 1 **tsp. sugar**
> ¼ **cup melted shortening**
> 5 **tbsp. sugar**
> 1 **tbsp. salt**
> 2 **eggs**
> 1 **cup milk, scalded**
> 2½ **cups whole wheat flour**
> 3-3½ **cups white flour**

PROOF

In a 2 cup measure, pour 1 cup warm water. Add 1 teaspoon sugar, but do not stir. Slowly sprinkle 1 tablespoon yeast into the water, making sure each particle gets wet. Again, do not stir. Wait 10 minutes until the yeast is thick and foamy.

MIX

Combine the following ingredients in the bread bowl, 5 tablespoons sugar, 1 tablespoon salt, 2 eggs, 1 cup cooled milk, 2½ cups whole wheat flour. Stir in proof yeast and 1/4 cup cooled, melted shortening.

ADD FLOUR (slowly)

Add remaining flour, 1 cup at a time to make a moderate dough. Lightly coat the dough with flour before turning it out.

KNEAD

Lightly dust kneading surface with flour, turn dough onto it and knead for 10 minutes, until dough is smooth and elastic.

1ST RISING

Place dough in greased bowl, turn to grease the top and set on a warm, draft-free spot and allow to rise until double: 1½ hours.

SHAPE

Punch dough down, remove from bowl, knead lightly, cover, and allow to rest for 10 minutes. Divide into 16-20 even pieces and shape into rolls (page 38).

2ND RISING

Place in greased muffin tins and set in a warm, draft-free spot and allow to rise until double: 20-30 minutes.

BAKE

Bake in **400°F** oven for **10-15 minutes.** Cool immediately on a wire rack.

A Big Batch of Whole Wheat

oooooooooooooooooooooooooooooooooooooooo

Makes 6- 8" x 4" x 3" sandwich loaves.

      8 **cups warm water**
      2 **tbsp. sugar**
      2 **tbsp. yeast**
      2 **tbsp. salt**
      2 **eggs**
     ½ **cup blackstrap molasses
          or honey**
     ½ **cup melted shortening**
      9 **cups whole wheat flour**
  13-15 **cups white flour**

PROOF
In a bread bowl, pour 8 cups warm water. Add 2 tablespoons sugar, but do not stir. Slowly sprinkle 2 tablespoons yeast into the water, making sure each particle gets wet. Again, do not stir. Wait 10 minutes until the yeast is thick and foamy.

MIX
Add the following ingredients to your bread bowl, stirring well between each addition: 2 tablespoons salt, 2 eggs, 1/2 cup molasses, 9 cups whole wheat flour and 1/2 cup cooled, melted shortening.

ADD FLOUR (quickly)
Add the 13-15 cups white flour, 1 cup at a time, to maintain a moderately soft dough. Coat the dough with flour before turning it out.

KNEAD
Turn the dough out onto a floured surface and knead until elastic: 15-20 minutes.

1ST RISING
Place the dough in a greased bowl, turn to grease the top, set in a warm, draft-free spot to rise until double: 1½ hours.

SHAPE
Punch the dough down, turn it out onto a clean surface and knead for 2 minutes. Cut the dough into 6 pieces and shape each piece into a smooth ball. Let the dough rest for 5 minutes, then shape into regular sandwich loaves (page 16). Place in greased loaf pans.

2ND RISING
Set the loaf pans in a warm, draft-free spot and allow to rise until double: 30 minutes.

BAKE
Bake in oven at **400°F** for **30 minutes.** Rotate the bread around in the oven half-way through baking to brown the crusts evenly. Cool immediately after baking on a wire rack.

Whole Wheat Pizza

○○○

Makes 1 Pizza

1 **tbsp. yeast**
1¼ **cups warm water**
1 **tsp. sugar**
1½ **tsp. salt**
3 **cups whole wheat flour**

PROOF

Pour 1¼ cups warm water into your bread bowl, add 1 teaspoon sugar and slowly sprinkle 1 tablespoon yeast into the water so that all of the particles are wet. Wait 10 minutes until the yeast is thick and foamy.

MIX

When the yeast has proofed add the following ingredients to your bread bowl, stirring well between each addition: 1½ teaspoons salt, 3 cups flour. Coat the dough with flour before turning it out.

KNEAD

Turn the dough out onto a lightly floured surface and knead until elastic: 5 minutes.

ONLY RISING

Place the dough in a greased bowl, turn to grease the top, set in a warm, draft-free spot to rise until double: 1 hour.

SHAPE

Punch the dough down and knead all of the large bubbles out of it. Place the dough on an oiled pizza pan and spread it out to the edges. If the dough will not spread easily, let it rest for a few minutes. Pinch the edges of the dough to stop the toppings from dripping off.

SAUCE: See Italian dough (page 65).

TOPPINGS:

1 **cup mozzerella cheese**
1 **cup shredded zucchini**
½ **cup chopped olives**
½ **cup chopped onions**
1 **tomato, thinly sliced**

Carmelite Bread

⊙⊙

A tasty, easy to digest bread, that adds bulk to your diet.

Makes 2- 8" x 4" x 3" sandwich loaves.

- ½ **cup warm water**
- 1 **tsp. sugar**
- 1½ **tbsp. yeast**
- 2 **cups warm water**
- ¼ **cup honey**
- 2 **tsp. salt**
- 1 **cup first break (or cracked wheat)**
- ¼ **cup flax seed**
- 1 **cup bran**
- 1 **cup whole wheat flour**
- ¼ **cup melted shortening**
- 4½-5 **cups flour**

PROOF
In a 1 cup measure, pour 1/2 cup warm water. Add 1 teaspoon sugar, but do not stir. Slowly sprinkle 1½ tablespoons yeast into the water, making sure each particle gets wet. Again, do not stir. Wait 10 minutes until the yeast is thick and foamy.

MIX
Meanwhile, in your bread bowl, add 2 cups warm water, 1/4 cup honey and stir to dissolve. Then add 2 teaspoons salt, 1 cup first break, 1/4 cup flax seed, 1 cup bran, 1 cup whole wheat flour and the proofed yeast. Stir well and add the 1/4 cup cooled, melted shortening.

ADD FLOUR (slowly)
Now add 4½-5 cups flour, 1 cup at a time, stirring well between each addition. The dough should feel rather soft and sticky. Coat the dough with flour before turning it out.

KNEAD
Flour your kneading surface, turn the dough out onto it and knead for 10 minutes. Lightly flour the dough if it becomes too sticky.

1ST RISING
When the dough feels elastic place it into a greased bowl, turn to grease the top, set in a warm, draft-free spot to rise until double: 1½ hours.

SHAPE
Then punch the dough down, turn it out onto a clean kneading surface. Knead it briefly so that the surface becomes very smooth. Cut the dough in half. Shape as you would a sticky dough (page 18), place the dough seam side down into a loaf pan. Set in a warm, draft-free spot and allow to double in bulk: 30 minutes.

BAKE
Bake in a **400°F** oven for **30 minutes.** Cool on a wire rack.

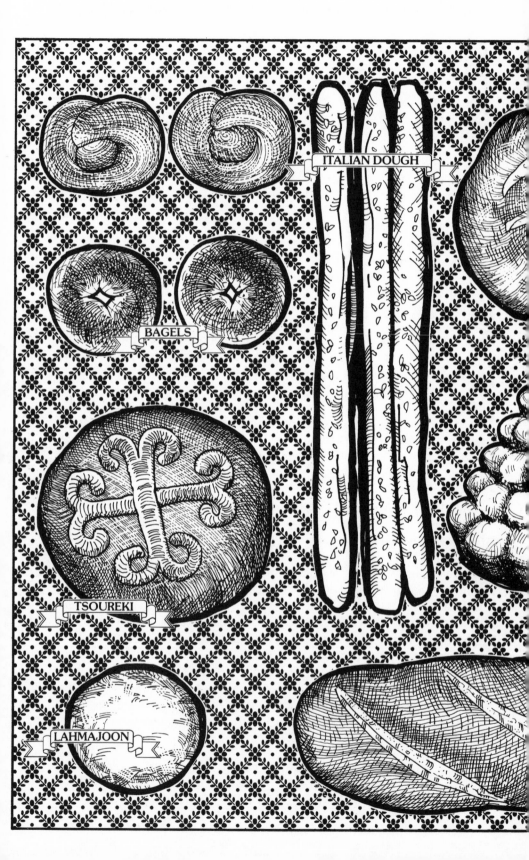

ITALIAN DOUGH

BAGELS

TSOUREKI

LAHMAJOON

INTERNATIONAL BREADS

SOFT PRETZELS

SAFFRON LUCIA BUNS

PANE DI MONREALE

ENGLISH MUFFINS

FRENCH BREAD

VIENNA LOAF

Vienna Loaf

⊙⊙⊙

My first success! I hope that it will be yours too.

Makes 2 free form loaves.

1¾ **cups warm water**	⅓ **cup skim milk powder**
1 **tsp. sugar**	2 **tsp. salt**
1 **tbsp. yeast**	2 **tbsp. melted shortening**
2 **tbsp. sugar**	5 **cups flour**

PROOF
In a 3 cup measure or small bowl, pour 1¾ cups warm water. Add 1 teaspoon sugar, but do not stir. Slowly sprinkle 1 tablespoon yeast into the water, making sure each particle gets wet. Again, do not stir. Wait 10 minutes until the yeast is thick and foamy.

MIX
While you are waiting, add the following ingredients to your bread bowl, stirring well between each addition: 2 tablespoons sugar, 1/3 cup skim milk powder, 2 teaspoons salt, the yeast, 1 cup flour and 2 tablespoons melted shortening.

ADD FLOUR (quickly)
Add remaining flour 1 cup at a time to make a stiff dough.

KNEAD
Turn the dough out onto a very lightly floured surface and knead until smooth and elastic: 10 minutes.

1ST RISING
Place the dough in a greased bowl, turn to grease the top, place in a warm, draft-free spot until double: 1½ hours.

SHAPE
See French Loaves, page 20. When shaped place on a greased baking sheet.

2ND RISING
Place the dough in a warm, draft-free spot for 30-40 minutes, or until double in bulk.

EGG WASH
Brush the dough with egg wash, (page 21) just before baking.

BAKE
Slash the top of each loaf diagonally 3 times before baking in a **400°F** oven for **30 minutes.** Cool on a wire rack immediately after baking.

If the dough gets sticky during kneading, powder it's "bottom" with 1 teaspoon flour. Continue kneading with only light powderings.

French Bread

⊙◎◎◎◎◎◎◎◎◎◎◎◎◎◎◎◎◎◎◎◎◎◎◎◎◎◎◎◎◎◎◎◎◎◎◎◎◎◎◎

Professional bakers can make this bread nice and crisp because their ovens have jets that spray steam during baking. You can try using clay tiles, bricks soaked in water, bowls of boiling water, or spraying with a plant mister but the results are never exactly the same. So what? I have seen my students make french bread that would make a pro envious and they used the following recipe. Makes 2-4 free form loaves.

2½ **cups warm water**
2 **tbsp. sugar**
1 **tbsp. yeast**

1 **tbsp. salt**
7 **cups flour**

PROOF
In a bread bowl, pour 2½ cups warm water. Add 2 tablespoons sugar, but do not stir. Slowly sprinkle 1 tablespoon yeast into the water, making sure each particle gets wet. Again, do not stir. Wait 10 minutes until the yeast is thick and foamy. Add 1 tablespoon salt.

ADD FLOUR (quickly)
Add flour 2 cups at a time to make a stiff dough.

KNEAD
Turn the dough out onto a lightly floured surface and knead until smooth and elastic: 10-12 minutes.

1ST RISING:
Place the dough in a greased bowl, turn to grease the top, place in a warm, draft-free spot, allow to rise until double in bulk: 1½-2 hours.

SHAPE
Turn the dough out onto a clean surface and cut in half. Knead each half into a smooth ball and wait 10 minutes until it is relaxed and very easy to work with. See page 20 for shaping instructions. Place dough on a greased baking sheet or a baking sheet that has been sprinkled with cornmeal. (Sprinkle cornmeal only where the dough will sit.)

2ND RISING
Allow to rise in a warm, draft-free spot until double: 30-45 minutes. If the dough spreads out sideways instead of reaching for the sky you've either let it over rise or your dough was too soft.

BAKE
Slash each loaf diagonally 3 times just before baking. Then bake in a **400°F** oven for **30 minutes.** I have found that the loaves are nicer if you spray them 3 times every 5 minutes during baking with a plant mister. Cool on a wire rack immediately after baking.

Note: Oil acts as a preservative. Because there isn't any in this recipe, you must either eat it the same day that you have baked it or freeze it immediately after it cools. If 2 loaves are too large for your purposes make 3 or even 4 smaller ones.

Remember that dough will double in size... Don't set them too close to one another during 2nd Rising. They may fall when you try to separate them.

Italian Dough

⊙⊙⊙⊙⊙⊙⊙⊙⊙⊙⊙⊙⊙⊙⊙⊙⊙⊙⊙⊙⊙⊙⊙⊙⊙⊙⊙⊙⊙⊙⊙⊙⊙⊙⊙⊙⊙⊙

A basic dough with 101 uses.

4 **cups warm water**	1 **tbsp. salt**
1 **tbsp. sugar**	¼ **cup olive oil**
2 **tbsp. yeast**	10-11 **cups flour**

PROOF

In a bread bowl, pour 4 cups warm water. Add 1 tablespoon sugar, but do not stir. Slowly sprinkle 2 tablespoons yeast into the water, making sure each particle gets wet. Again, do not stir. Wait 10 minutes until the yeast is thick and foamy.

MIX

Mix in 1 tablespoon salt and 2 cups flour. Stir in 1/4 cup oil.

ADD FLOUR (quickly)

Add remaining flour, 2 cups at a time to make a moderately stiff dough. If you will be using this for only pizza dough make a soft dough. Coat the dough lightly with flour before turning it out.

KNEAD

Turn the dough out onto a lightly floured surface and knead until smooth and elastic: 10-12 minutes.

1ST RISING

Place dough in a greased bowl, turn to grease the top, place in a warm spot and allow to rise until double: 1½ hours.

SHAPE

This recipe is big so you can make a few of the following, as you require. After punching the dough down, knead it for 2 minutes and then let it rest for 5-10 minutes.

Buns: Makes 12-18 hero sandwich buns or 24 dinner rolls. So good with spaghetti or lasagna. Roll the dough out into a long rope and cut it into the desired number of pieces. Let the dough rest before shaping. Now roll each piece into a short rope and tie it into a knot. Place it on a greased baking sheet.

Loaves: Makes 2 or 3. Cut the dough into the desired number of pieces. Shape each into a smooth ball and place either on a greased baking sheet or on a baking sheet that has been sprinkled with cornmeal. (Sprinkle cornmeal only where the loaves will sit.) Or roll each piece into a short, fat rope. Place on a greased baking sheet, seam side down.

Italian Dough (continued)

⊙⊙

Bread Sticks: It will take a big of experimentation to discover which type of breadstick that you want to make. Do you want them short, fat and chewy, or long, thin, and crisp? Simply cut the dough into the number of sticks that you want (don't use all of it!). After the dough has rested roll each piece into a rope of the desired length and thickness. Place on a greased baking sheet. Let them rise for 10-20 minutes. Brush with egg wash (page 21) and sprinkle with sesame seeds, poppy seeds or coarse salt.

Pizza: This dough makes 4- 18" pizzas with a nice thick crust. Cut the dough in 4 and shape each quarter into a smooth ball, let them rest. Place each ball in the middle of an oiled pizza pan. The oil helps with the shaping. Press down on the dough to flatten it out. If the dough becomes too elastic let it rest then try again. Make the crust on the edge of the pan thicker so that the toppings will not fall off during baking.

TOPPING: (Sauce)
- 7½ **oz. tomato sauce**
- 1 **clove garlic, minced**
- 1 **small onion, chopped fine**
- 1 **tsp. basil**
- ½ **tsp. oregano**

Simmer for 20 minutes until slightly thickened. Grate ½-¾ lb. Mozzerella cheese and spread it over the sauce.

- ½ **cup pepperoni, sliced**
- ¼ **green pepper, diced**
- ½ **cup cooked bacon, drained**
  Anchovies, olives, fresh tomatoes, pineapple and ham (optional)

2ND RISING
Buns: 30 minutes.
Bread Sticks: 10-20 minutes, depending on how crisp you like them.
Bread: 30-40 minutes, slash the tops before baking.
Pizza: None, bake after topping has been added.

BAKE
Buns: **400°F** for **20-25 minutes.**
Bread Sticks: **375°F** for **15 minutes.**
Bread: **400°F** for **30-35 minutes.**
Pizza: **450°F** for **25 minutes,** until it can be easily lifted from the pan.

Making bread is like riding a bicycle - once you've mastered it you never forget it, but the first few attempts are likely to end in failure.

Saffron Lucia Buns

⊙⊙⊙⊙⊙⊙⊙⊙⊙⊙⊙⊙⊙⊙⊙⊙⊙⊙⊙⊙⊙⊙⊙⊙⊙⊙⊙⊙⊙⊙⊙⊙⊙⊙⊙

- ½ **cup warm water**
- 1 **tsp. sugar**
- 2 **tbsp. yeast**
- 1 **tsp. saffron**
- 2 **tbsp. boiling water**
- ¾ **cup milk, scalded**
- 1 **egg**
- ⅓ **cup sugar**
- 1 **tsp. salt**
- ¼ **cup melted margarine**
- 3½ **cups flour**

Combine the saffron and boiling water and allow to cool.

PROOF
In a 1 cup measure, pour 1/2 cup warm water. Add 1 teaspoon sugar, but do not stir. Slowly sprinkle 2 tablespoons yeast into the water, making sure each particle gets wet. Again, do not stir. Wait 10 minutes until the yeast is thick and foamy.

MIX
Add the following ingredients to your bread bowl, stirring well between each addition: 3/4 cup lukewarm milk, the saffron, 1 egg, 1/3 cup sugar, 1 teaspoon salt, the yeast, 1 cup flour and 1/4 cup cooled, melted margarine.

ADD FLOUR (slowly)
Add remaining flour 1 cup at a time to make a soft dough. Coat the dough lightly with flour before turning it out.

KNEAD
Turn the dough out onto a lightly floured surface and knead until smooth and elastic: 8 minutes.

1ST RISING
Place the dough in a greased bowl, set in a warm, draft-free spot, allow to rise until double: 1½ hours.

SHAPE
Punch the dough down and turn it out onto a clean surface. Roll the dough into an 18" long strip and cut into 18 pieces. Roll each piece into a strip 10"-12" long and cut it in half. Coil both ends of each strip into the center of the strip. Place 2 coiled strips back to back to make 1 bun. Press a raisin into the center of each coil. Place on a greased baking sheet.

Saffron Lucia Buns (continued)

2ND RISING
Set the baking sheet in a warm, draft-free spot and allow to rise until double: 30 minutes.

EGG WASH
Just before baking, brush the buns with egg wash, page 21. Then combine 1/4 cup finely chopped almonds with 2 tablespoons sugar. Sprinkle a little of the mixture onto each bun.

BAKE
Bake in a **375°F** oven for **20 minutes,** until golden.

Lahmajoon (Armenian Meat Pies)

○○

These delicious little finger foods freeze well. Make the entire batch now, freeze some for a quick meal later.

Serves 12.

DOUGH:
⅓ **cup warm water**
1 **tsp. sugar**
1 **tbsp. yeast**
1 **cup milk, scalded**
1 **tsp. salt**
1 **tbsp. sugar**
¼ **cup melted margarine**
4 **cups flour**

PROOF
In a bread bowl, pour 1/3 cup warm water. Add 1 teaspoon sugar, but do not stir. Slowly sprinkle 1 tablespoon yeast into the water, making sure each particle gets wet. Again, do not stir. Wait 10 minutes until the yeast is thick and foamy.

MIX
After the yeast has proofed, add the following ingredients to your bread bowl, stirring well between each addition: 1 cup milk, cooled, 1 teaspoon salt, 1 tablespoon sugar, 1 cup flour, 1/4 cup cooled margarine.

ADD FLOUR (slowly)
Add remaining flour 1 cup at a time to make a soft dough. Coat the dough with flour before turning it out.

KNEAD
Turn the dough out onto a lightly floured surface and knead until smooth and elastic: 8 minutes.

1ST RISING
Place the dough in a greased bowl, turn to grease the top, set in a warm, draft-free spot until doubled: 1½ hours.
MIX THE FILLING WHILE YOU ARE WAITING
FILLING:

2 **lbs. ground beef or lamb**	1 **can Italian tomatoes**
½ **cup chopped parsley**	⅛ **tsp. pepper**
1 **green pepper, minced**	1 **tbsp. mint, if using lamb**
1 **large onion, minced**	**dash cayenne papper**
1 **garlic clove, minced**	

Lahmajoon (continued)

SHAPE

Punch the dough down and turn it out onto a clean surface. Roll it into a 32" rope. Cut it into 32 pieces. Roll each piece into a 5-6" circle. Arrange as many circles as you can on a baking sheet. Place some of the meat mixture on each piece and spread it evenly, leaving a 1/4" margin around the edges.

BAKE

Preheat the oven to **450°F.** Place 1 oven rack at the bottom of the oven, and the other rack as high as you can in the oven. Place the baking sheet on the lower rack for **6-8 minutes,** then move the sheet to the upper rack for **5 more minutes,** until the lahmajoon browns lightly. Continue preparing and baking the balance of the pies. Lahmajoon keeps very well in the freezer.

To reheat the frozen lahmajoons, arrange them on a baking sheet, and place 1 face up and 1 face down on top of it to keep the filling from drying out. Bake them at 400°F for 15 minutes.

English Muffins

⊙⊙⊙

These are different because you cook them in a frying pan that has been sprinkled with cornmeal instead of baking them in the oven. Split them with a fork, smother them in butter and serve with homemade strawberry jam - delicious!

Makes 12- 2" muffins.

1 **cup warm water**	1 **egg**
1 **tsp. sugar**	1½ **tsp. salt**
1 **tbsp. yeast**	3 **tbsp. melted margarine**
3 **tbsp. sugar**	3 **cups flour**
½ **cup skim milk powder**	**cornmeal**

PROOF
In a bread bowl, pour 1 cup warm water. Add 1 teaspoon sugar, but do not stir. Slowly sprinkle 1 tablespoon yeast into the water, making sure each particle gets wet. Again, do not stir. Wait 10 minutes until the yeast is thick and foamy.

MIX
Then add the following ingredients, stirring well between each addition: 3 tablespoons sugar, 1/2 cup skim milk powder, 1 egg, 1½ teaspoons salt, 1 cup flour, 3 tablespoons melted margarine.

ADD FLOUR (slowly)
Add flour 1/2 cup at a time to retain a soft dough. Coat the dough lightly with flour before turning it out.

KNEAD
Turn the dough out onto a lightly floured surface and knead until smooth and elastic: 8 minutes.

1ST RISING
Place the dough in a greased bowl, turn to grease the top, set in a warm, draft-free spot, allow to rise until double: 1½ hours.

SHAPE
Turn the dough out onto a clean surface and with a rolling pin roll it into a rectangle that is 1/2" thick. Let the dough rest for a minute, and then cut it out with a 2" cookie cutter. Place the muffins on an ungreased cookie sheet that has been sprinkled with cornmeal. Continue gathering the dough up and rolling it out until all of the dough has been used up.

2ND RISING
Place the cookie sheet in a warm, draft-free spot and allow to rise until double: 30 minutes.

COOK
Sprinkle an electric frying pan or griddle with cornmeal after preheating it to **350°F**. Place the muffins on the cornmeal and cook for **10 minutes** on each side. Serve warm.

Soft Pretzels

1¼ **cup warm water**
1 **tbsp. yeast**
1 **tsp. sugar**
2 **tsp. salt**
4 **cups flour**

PROOF
In a bread bowl, pour 1¼ cups warm water. Add 1 teaspoon sugar, but do not stir. Slowly sprinkle 1 tablespoon yeast into the water, making sure each particle gets wet. Again, do not stir. Wait 10 minutes until the yeast is thick and foamy.

MIX
When the yeast has proofed, add 2 teaspoons salt and stir.

ADD FLOUR (slowly)
Add 4 cups flour, 1 cup at a time. The dough should be stiff.

KNEAD
Turn dough out onto the kneading surface and knead until smooth and elastic: 8 minutes. Place dough into a greased bowl, turn to grease the top, set in a warm, draft-free spot and allow to rise until double: 1½ hours.

SHAPE
When double, punch dough down, turn out and knead briefly. Roll dough into a short rope and cut it into 24 pieces. Roll each piece into a rope - 10" long. Shape into pretzels and put aside on an ungreased cookie sheet. When all the pretzels are shaped you can broil them for 1 minute on each side, as a result they will be golden brown when baked.

In a saucepan bring 4 cups of water to a boil. Reduce heat to simmer. Add pretzels, 3 at a time, to the water. When they become puffy (in about 30 seconds) remove and drain well on a rack.

When all of the pretzels have been immersed and drained, place them on a greased baking sheet.

EGG WASH
Brush with egg wash (page 21) and sprinkle with coarse salt.

BAKE
Bake in a **475°F** oven for **15 minutes.**

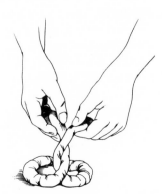

Bagels

Oooooooooooooooooooooooooooooooooooooooooo

Bagels are the most time consuming of all breads. The results, though, are well worth the effort.

Makes 12 bagels.

2 **tbsp. yeast**	4¼-4½ **cups flour**
1½ **cups warm water**	3 **tbsp. sugar**
1 **tsp. sugar**	1 **tbsp. salt**

PROOF
In a bread bowl, pour 1½ cups warm water. Add 1 teaspoon sugar, but do not stir. Slowly sprinkle 2 tablespoons yeast into the water, making sure each particle gets wet. Again, do not stir. Wait 10 minutes until the yeast is thick and foamy.

MIX
Add 3 tablespoons sugar, 1 tablespoon salt and 1 cup flour. (Do not add oil to bagels, they lose their characteristic texture.) Stir until smooth.

ADD FLOUR (quickly)
Add remaining flour, 1 cup at a time, to make a moderately stiff dough.

KNEAD
Turn out and knead until smooth and elastic. Cover and let dough rest for 10 minutes.

SHAPE
Cut into 12 portions; shape into smooth balls. Punch hole in center of each with a floured finger. Twirl gently to enlarge hole. Place on an ungreased baking sheet.

ONLY RISING
Cover and set in a warm, draft-free spot and let rise for 20 minutes.

Place raised bagels under broiler until they start to brown, turn over and brown other side: 1-2 minutes. Set a large pot of water and 1 tablespoon sugar to boil, reduce the heat to minimum setting. Place 4 bagels in water and turn after 30 seconds. If you leave them in too long they will wrinkle. Remove bagels and drain on a rack for 10 minutes.

BAKE
When all bagels have been well drained, place on a greased baking sheet and bake in a **375°F** oven for **30-35 minutes.** Cool on a rack.

Note: Because there isn't any oil in this recipe, bagels do not last very long. If they will not be eaten in 2 days, freeze them.

Pane Di Monreale (Sicily)

⊙⊙⊙

Makes 1 loaf.

- ¾ **cup warm water**
- 1 **tsp. sugar**
- 2 **tbsp. yeast**
- 1 **cup milk, scalded**
- 2 **tsp. salt**
- 1 **tbsp. sugar**
- 2 **tbsp. oil**
- 1 **tsp. ground mahlepi**
- 5 **cups flour**

PROOF
In a 2 cup measure, pour 3/4 cup warm water. Add 1 teaspoon sugar, but do not stir. Slowly sprinkle 2 tablespoons yeast into the water, making sure each particle gets wet. Again, do not stir. Wait 10 minutes until the yeast is thick and foamy.

MIX
Meanwhile, in your bread bowl add 1 cup cooled, scalded milk, 2 teaspoons salt, 1 tablespoon sugar and 1 teaspoon ground mahlepi. When yeast has proofed pour it into the bread bowl with 1 cup flour. Stir well, then add the 2 tablespoons oil.

ADD FLOUR (quickly)
Add remaining flour 1 cup at a time so that the dough is rather stiff.

KNEAD
Turn out, knead until smooth and elastic: 10 minutes.

1ST RISING
Place dough into a greased bowl, turn to grease the top, place in a warm, draft-free spot and allow to rise until double in bulk: 1½ hours.

SHAPE
When dough has doubled, punch it down, turn it out, and knead briefly. Cover with a towel and allow it to rest until it is easy to work with. Roll the dough out into 1 rope 30" x 2½" long. Allow the dough to rest if it becomes too difficult to roll. Then cut the rope into three lengths: small, medium and large. Coil the large rope, tucking the end underneath, and place it onto a greased baking sheet. Coil the remaining ropes, and place them onto the largest coil. Make sure they are properly centered so they won't fall off.

2ND RISING
Place in a warm, draft-free spot for 30 minutes.

BAKE
With kitchen shears, cut slits 1" apart around each coil and spread apart if necessary. Brush with egg wash (page 21) and bake in a **400°F** oven for **40 minutes,** watching that it does not burn during the last 10 minutes. Remove from the oven and cool on a wire rack.

Tsoureki (Greece)

○○○

A Greek treat that is sure to please. Malhepi is an expensive spice that can be purchased in a Greek specialty shop. If you can't find it omit it, but you will be missing a wonderful taste experience.

Makes 2 loaves.

SEASONING:

½ **tsp. cinnamon**	1 **bay leaf**
½ **tsp. anise seed**	¼ **tsp. mahlepi**
½ **tsp. orange peel**	½ **cup water**

Combine the 5 seasoning ingredients in a small saucepan. Add 1/2 cup water and bring the mixture to a boil. Remove from heat and allow to steep and cool.

DOUGH:

¼ **cup water**	½ **cup sugar**
1 **tsp. sugar**	½ **tsp. salt**
1½ **tbsp. yeast**	5-6 **cups flour**
½ **cup milk, scalded**	¼ **cup melted butter**
3 **eggs**	

PROOF

In a 1 cup measure, pour 1/4 cup warm water. Add 1 teaspoon sugar, but do not stir. Slowly sprinkle 1½ tablespoons yeast into the water, making sure each particle gets wet. Again, do not stir. Wait 10 minutes until the yeast is thick and foamy.

MIX

Add the following ingredients to your bread bowl, stirring well between each addition: 1/2 cup cooled milk, 3 eggs, 1/2 cup sugar, 1/2 teaspoon salt, the yeast, 1 cup flour, 1/4 cup lukewarm butter, and all seasonings.

ADD FLOUR (quickly)

Add remaining flour 1 cup at a time to make a moderately stiff dough. Coat the dough lightly with flour before turning it out.

KNEAD

Turn the dough out onto a lightly floured surface and knead until smooth and elastic: 10 minutes.

Tsoureki (continued)

1ST RISING
Place the dough in a greased bowl, turn to grease the top, set in a warm, draft-free spot until double: 1½-2 hours.

SHAPE
Punch the dough down and turn it out onto a clean surface. Divide the dough in half. Pinch off 2 pieces from each half the size of a walnut and set aside. Shape each half into a round loaf and place on a greased baking sheet. BYZANTINE CROSS: Roll each extra piece into a long rope 12-14" long. Slit the ends down 5". Coil each slit in opposite directions. Place on loaf. Form a cross with the 2 ropes. Do not press flat.

2ND RISING
Set the baking sheets in a warm, draft-free spot, allow to rise until double: 30-45 minutes.

EGG WASH
Brush with egg wash (page 21) immediately before baking. Also before you bake you can decorate the cross with walnut or cherry halves.

BAKE
Bake at **375°F** for **40-45 minutes.**

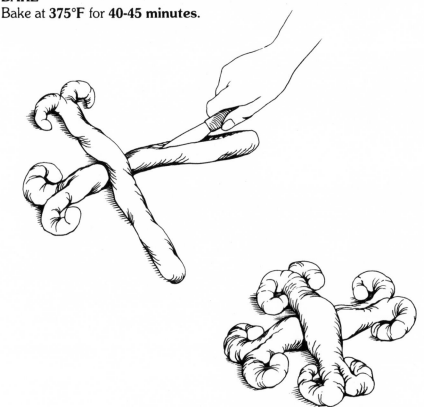

Place Byzantine cross on top of round loaf.

MEAL-IN-A-LOAF

JEAN'S CHICKEN
SQUARES

DELI SPECIAL
BAKED REUBEN

MEALS, SNACKS AND HORS D'OEUVRES

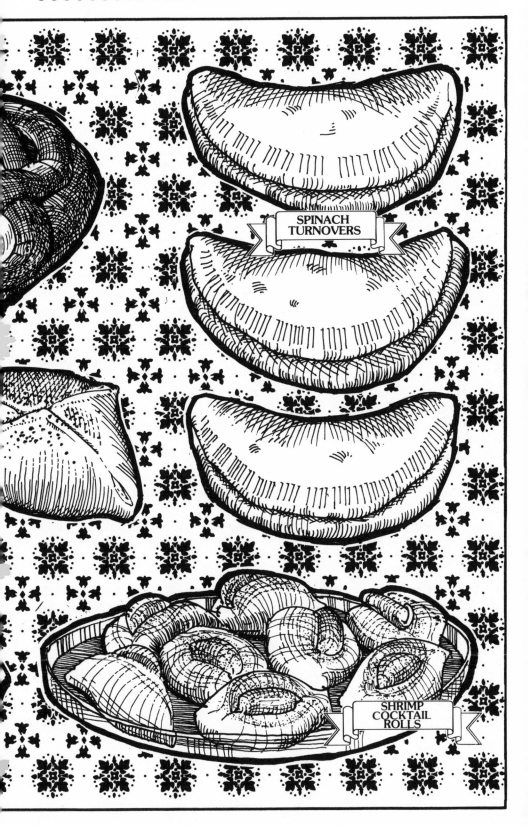

SPINACH TURNOVERS

SHRIMP COCKTAIL ROLLS

Jean's Chicken Squares

◉◉

Make a delicious meal with leftover chicken.

DOUGH:

⅓ **cup warm water**	1½ **tsp. salt**
1 **tsp. sugar**	2 **tbsp. melted margarine**
1 **tbsp. yeast**	½ **cup onion, finely chopped**
½ **cup milk (scalded)**	2½ **cups flour**
2 **tbsp. sugar**	

FILLING:

3½ **oz. cream cheese with pimento**	¼ **tsp. salt**
2 **tbsp. melted butter**	⅛ **tsp. pepper**
2 **cups chicken, cooked and cubed**	2 **tbsp. milk**
	1 **tbsp. chopped chives**

PROOF

In a 1 cup measure, pour 1/3 cup warm water. Add 1 teaspoon sugar, but do not stir. Slowly sprinkle 1 tablespoon yeast into the water, making sure each particle gets wet. Again, do not stir. Wait 10 minutes until the yeast is thick and foamy.

MIX

In your bread bowl, or a small mixing bowl, add 1/2 cup milk (cooled), 2 tablespoons sugar, 1½ teaspoons salt. Add the yeast and 1 cup of the flour. Then add 1/2 cup finely chopped onion and 2 tablespoons melted margarine.

ADD FLOUR (quickly)

Add the remaining flour to obtain a stiff dough. If the dough is too moist, lightly coat it with flour before turning it out.

KNEAD

Turn the dough out onto a very lightly floured surface and knead for 5 minutes. Cover the dough with a dry tea towel and allow it to rest for 15 minutes.

Prepare the filling by combining all of the filling ingredients and mixing well to evenly coat the chicken cubes. Add more milk if the mixture seems too dry.

SHAPE

Roll the dough into a 12" x 16" rectangle. If the dough is very elastic and will not roll easily, let it rest for another minute and try again, it should be easier to work with. Cut the dough into 12- 4" squares. Evenly distribute the filling into the middle of each square. Now take the corners of one of the squares and bring them into the middle of the filling. Seal the seams with deep pinches for a fluted effect. Place the squares on a cookie sheet. Brush with egg wash and sprinkle with poppy or sesame seeds.

BAKE

Bake for **20-25 minutes** in a **350°F** oven.

Serve hot or cold with a tossed salad.

Deli Special Baked Reuben

⊙⊙

A no-knead recipe.

Makes 1- 9" square cake pan.

> 1 **cup warm water**
> 1 **tsp. sugar**
> 1 **tbsp. yeast**
> 1 **tbsp. onion, chopped**
> 1½ **tsp. caraway seeds**
> 1 **tsp. salt**
> 2 **tbsp. molasses**
> 2 **tbsp. oil**
> 1 **cup rye flour**
> 1 **cup flour**
> ¼ **cup mayonnaise**
> 2 **tsp. mustard**

PROOF

In a bread bowl, pour 1 cup warm water. Add 1 teaspoon sugar, but do not stir. Slowly sprinkle 1 tablespoon yeast into the water, making sure each particle gets wet. Again, do not stir. Wait 10 minutes until the yeast is thick and foamy.

MIX

Then add the following, stirring after each addition: 1 tablespoon onion, 1½ teaspoons caraway seeds, 1 teaspoon salt, 2 tablespoons molasses, 2 tablespoons oil, 1 cup rye flour and 1 cup flour.

Grease the cake pan and pour the batter into it, spread it out evenly. If the dough is too sticky to spread, lightly coat it with flour and continue spreading.

Combine 1/4 cup mayonnaise and 2 teaspoons mustard. Spread over the batter and let rise until doubled. Be careful that it does not rise over the top of the pan.

> TOPPING:
> ½ **lb. sliced corned beef,**
>   **chopped**
> 8 **oz. sauerkraut, drained**
> 4 **oz. sliced Swiss Cheese**

Sprinkle the risen dough with sauerkraut, then sprinkle with the corned beef. Top with cheese slices.

BAKE

Bake in a **375°F** oven for **30-35 minutes**. Serve.

Shrimp Cocktail Rolls

⊙⊙

These little rolls make delightful hors d'oeuvres.

1 **cup warm water**	2½ **cups flour**
1 **tsp. sugar**	6 **oz. small shrimp**
1 **tbsp. yeast**	2 **tbsp. parmesan cheese**
⅓ **skim milk powder**	1 **tbsp. cornmeal**
1 **tsp. salt**	**melted butter**
1 **tbsp. horseradish**	**shrimp sauce**
3 **tbsp. oil**	

PROOF

In a bread bowl, pour 1 cup warm water. Add 1 teaspoon sugar, but do not stir. Slowly sprinkle 1 tablespoon yeast into the water, making sure each particle gets wet. Again, do not stir. Wait 10 minutes until the yeast is thick and foamy.

MIX

Then stir in 1/3 cup skim milk powder, 1 teaspoon salt, 1 tablespoon horseradish, 1 cup flour and 3 tablespoons oil. Stir well.

ADD FLOUR (slowly)

Add the remaining flour, 1/2 cup at a time to make a soft dough. Coat the dough lightly with flour before turning it out.

KNEAD

Turn the dough out and knead for 8 minutes, until smooth and elastic. Allow to rest for 10 minutes.

SHAPE

Roll the dough out to 1/4" thickness and cut into 2" circles. Make a crease slightly off center, across each circle. Place 1/4 teaspoon shrimp sauce on each circle.

Place 1 shrimp on the larger side of each round. Fold over small side so back of shrimp shows. Press edges together well to seal. Twist each end once or twice. Place on greased baking sheets. Curve ends slightly to resemble a shell; press ends flat with a floured fork.

ONLY RISING

Set in a warm, draft-free spot and allow to rise until double in bulk: 20-30 minutes. Brush the rolls with melted butter. Combine 2 tablespoons parmesan cheese and 1 tablespoon cornmeal and sprinkle over rolls.

BAKE

Bake in a **375°F** oven for **15-20 minutes,** until golden brown. Serve warm.

Spinach Turnovers

⊙⊙

DOUGH:

1 **cup warm water**	1 **egg**
1 **tsp. sugar**	1 **cup flour**
2 **tbsp. yeast**	½ **cup melted margarine**
2 **tbsp. sugar**	2½ **cups flour**
1 **tsp. salt**	

PROOF

In a bread bowl, pour 1 cup warm water. Add 1 teaspoon sugar, but do not stir. Slowly sprinkle 2 tablespoons yeast into the water, making sure each particle gets wet. Again, do not stir. Wait 10 minutes until the yeast is thick and foamy.

MIX

Then add the following ingredients, stirring well between each addition: 2 tablespoons sugar, 1 teaspoon salt, 1 egg, 1 cup flour, 1/2 cup cooled, melted margarine and 2½ cups flour.

KNEAD

Lightly coat the dough with flour and turn it out onto a lightly floured kneading surface. Knead until smooth and elastic: 10 minutes.

1ST RISING

Place in a greased bowl, turn to grease the top, set in a warm, draft-free spot and allow to rise until double: 1½ hours.

Combine the filling and set aside.

FILLING:

1 **cup Romano or Parmesan cheese**	1 **cup chopped spinach, cooked and well drained**
1 **cup Mozzarella cheese, grated**	2 **eggs**

SHAPE

When the dough has doubled punch it down and turn it out. Roll it into a 30" long rope and cut it into 1" pieces. With a rolling pin, roll each piece into a 4" circle, on a floured surface. Place 1 tablespoon of filling on each circle. Fold half of the circle over the filling and seal with a fork. Place on a greased baking sheet. Brush with egg wash if desired (page 21).

BAKE

Bake in a **400°F** oven for **15-18 minutes.** Serve warm.

Meal-In-A-Loaf

ⓞⓞⓞⓞⓞⓞⓞⓞⓞⓞⓞⓞⓞⓞⓞⓞⓞⓞⓞⓞⓞⓞⓞⓞⓞⓞⓞⓞⓞⓞⓞⓞⓞⓞⓞⓞⓞⓞ

This loaf is delicious when served as either a hot or a cold meal. Serve it to the gang on Grey Cup day along with a raw vegetable dip.

DOUGH:

½ **cup warm water**	2 **tbsp. sugar**
1 **tsp. sugar**	1 **tbsp. salt**
1½ **tbsp. yeast**	3 **tbsp. melted margarine**
2 **cups milk, scalded**	6-6½ **cups flour**

PROOF

In a 1 cup measure, pour 1/2 cup warm water. Add 1 teaspoon sugar, but do not stir. Slowly sprinkle 1½ tablespoons yeast into the water, making sure each particle gets wet. Again, do not stir. Wait 10 minutes until the yeast is thick and foamy.

MIX

Meanwhile, in your bread bowl mix together 2 cups lukewarm milk, 2 tablespoons sugar and 1 tablespoon salt. Stir the yeast down with a fork and pour it into your bread bowl. Then stir in 1 cup of flour. Add 3 tablespoons melted margarine.

ADD FLOUR (slowly)

Add the remaining flour 1 cup at a time to make a medium soft dough. Lightly coat the dough with flour before turning it out.

KNEAD

Knead for 10 minutes. The dough should be very smooth and elastic with a slight tacky feeling to it.

1ST RISING

Place the dough into a greased bowl, turn the dough to grease the top. Set in a warm, draft-free spot and allow to rise until double: 1½ hours.

FILLING:

6 **oz. grated swiss cheese**	1 **lb. polish sausage or**
(or similar cheese)	**pepperoni**
4 **large eggs**	**large olives**

Meal-In-A-Loaf (continued)

⦿⦿⦿⦿⦿⦿⦿⦿⦿⦿⦿⦿⦿⦿⦿⦿⦿⦿⦿⦿⦿⦿⦿⦿⦿⦿⦿⦿⦿⦿⦿⦿⦿⦿⦿⦿⦿⦿⦿

SHAPE

When the dough has doubled, punch it down, turn it out, and gently knead for 1 minute. Shape it into a smooth ball and allow to rest. Grease a pizza pan. Cut the dough in half but make one half larger than the other. Roll the smaller half into a circle slightly smaller than your pizza pan. Place it on the pizza pan. Then put the cheese in the middle of the circle. Cut off 1/3 of the remaining dough and roll it into a circle large enough to cover the cheese but not as large as the first circle. Cover the cheese. Place the eggs, sausage and olives around the cheese.

Cut the remaining dough into five. Roll four pieces into a 24" long rope. Weave each rope around the eggs and olives and over the sausage. Making it appear continous. Roll the last piece of dough out to make a decoration in the center of the loaf.

2ND RISING

Cover and allow to rise for 20-30 minutes.

BAKE

Glaze with an egg wash (page 21) and bake in a **375°F** oven for **45 minutes**. Cool on a wire rack.

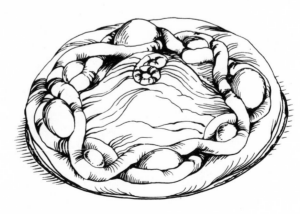

BEA'S BUTTER HORNS

THE THREE BEARS

CHELSEA BUNS

ALMOND PRETZEL COFFEE CAKE

FINNISH COFFEE BRAID

LEMON BRAID

APPLE RAISIN TWIST

RAISIN BREAD

TREATS
AND SWEETS

DATE NUT
COFFEE CAKE

FILLED
APPLE KUCHEN

SUNRISE
COFFEE CAKE

CLASSROOM
COFFEE CAKE

COFFEE BREAKERS

BAKED
DOUGHNUTS

Raisin Bread

◉◉◉

Makes 2- 8" x 4" x 3" loaves.

　½ **cup warm water**
　1 **tsp. sugar**
　2 **tbsp. yeast**
　1 **cup milk, scalded**
1½ **tsp. salt**
　½ **cup sugar**
　½ **cup melted margarine**
　1 **cup raisins**
　2 **eggs**
5½-6 **cups flour**

PROOF
In a 1 cup measure, pour 1/2 cup warm water. Add 1 teaspoon sugar, but do not stir. Slowly sprinkle 2 tablespoons yeast into the water, making sure each particle gets wet. Again, do not stir. Wait 10 minutes until the yeast is thick and foamy.

MIX
Meanwhile, using a whisk, mix the following ingredients in your bread bowl: 1 cup lukewarm milk, 1½ tsp. salt, 1/2 cup sugar, 2 eggs and 1 cup of flour. Whisk in the yeast, then the 1/2 cup cooled margarine. Add 1 cup raisins and stir with your wooden spoon.

ADD FLOUR (slowly)
Add the remaining flour, 1 cup at a time, to make a soft dough. Coat the dough with flour before turning it out onto the kneading surface.

KNEAD
Dust the kneading surface with flour and turn the dough out onto it. Then, dust your hands with flour and knead the dough for 10 minutes. Whenever the dough feels too sticky dust it and your hands with flour.

1ST RISING
After kneading, place the dough into a greased bowl, turn to grease the top, set in a warm, draft-free spot and allow to double: 2 hours.

SHAPE
Punch the dough down, knead it briefly and let it rest so that it will be easier to shape. Cut in half, shape into loaves (page 16), and place each loaf into a greased pan. Remember that exposed raisins will burn, so remove them. Set in a warm, draft-free spot and allow to double in a warm place: 45 minutes.

BAKE
Bake in a **400°F** oven for **10 minutes,** then turn the heat down to **375°F** for a further **20-25 minutes.**

Note: Before you bake this bread you can brush the tops with a mixture of melted margarine and cinnamon.

Classroom Coffee Cake

⊚○⊚

Makes 2.

¼ **cup warm water**	1 **tsp. lemon peel**
1 **tsp. sugar**	1 **tsp. vanilla**
1 **tbsp. yeast**	1 **tsp. salt**
1½ **cups milk, scalded**	½ **cup melted margarine**
2 **eggs**	5-5½ **cups flour**

PROOF
In a 1 cup measure, pour 1/4 cup warm water. Add 1 teaspoon sugar, but do not stir. Slowly sprinkle 1 tablespoon yeast into the water, making sure each particle gets wet. Again, do not stir. Wait 10 minutes until the yeast is thick and foamy.

MIX
Meanwhile add the following ingredients to your bread bowl, stirring well between each addition: 1½ cups warm milk, 2 eggs, 1 teaspoon lemon peel, 1 teaspoon vanilla, 1 teaspoon salt, the proofed yeast, 1 cup flour and 1/2 cup warm margarine.

ADD FLOUR (slowly)
Add flour 1 cup at a time to make a moderately soft dough. Coat the dough with flour before turning it out.

KNEAD
Turn the dough out onto a lightly floured surface and knead until smooth and elastic: 10 minutes.

1ST RISING
Place the dough in a greased bowl, turn to grease the top, set in a warm, draft-free spot, allow to rise until double: 1½ hours.

SHAPE
Punch the dough down and turn it out onto a clean surface. Cut the dough in half. Roll 1/2 into a 24" long rope. Coil it into a well greased 9" pie plate. Cut the remaining half into 9 pieces and shape each piece into a smooth ball. Place them, in circular fashion, in another well greased pie plate.

2ND RISING
Place the pie plates in a warm, draft-free spot and allow them to rise until double: 30-40 minutes.

EGG WASH
Brush with egg wash immediately before baking, (page 21).

BAKE
Bake in oven at **375°F** for **20-25 minutes.** Cool immediately after baking on a wire rack.

GLAZE
Cool and glaze with Icing Sugar Glaze (page 22). Decorate with slivered almonds or glacé cherries.

Reduce the heat by 50°F when using glass pans.

Sunrise Coffee Cake

Makes 2.

- ½ cup warm water
- 1 tsp. sugar
- 2 tbsp. yeast
- 1 cup milk (scalded)
- ½ cup sugar
- 2 eggs
- 1 tsp. lemon peel, grated
- 1 tsp. salt
- ½ cup melted margarine
- 5 cups flour
- jam or jelly

PROOF

In a 1 cup measure, pour 1/2 cup warm water. Add 1 teaspoon sugar, but do not stir. Slowly sprinkle 2 tablespoons yeast into the water, making sure each particle gets wet. Again, do not stir. Wait 10 minutes until the yeast is thick and foamy.

MIX

While you are waiting, add the following ingredients to your bread bowl, stirring well between each addition: 1 cup lukewarm milk, 2 eggs, 1/2 cup sugar, 1 teaspoon salt and 1 teaspoon lemon peel. Add the yeast. Stir in 1 cup of flour then 1/2 cup cooled, melted margarine.

ADD FLOUR (quickly)

Add remaining flour 1 cup at a time to make a stiff dough.

KNEAD

Turn the dough out onto a lightly floured surface and knead until smooth and elastic: 8-10 minutes.

1ST RISING

Place the dough in a greased bowl, turn to grease the top, place in a warm spot for 1½-2 hours.

SHAPE

Turn the dough out onto a clean surface and cut it in half. Roll 1/2 into a 10" x 8" rectangle using a little bit of flour if necessary. Using a doughnut cutter cut out twelve doughnuts. Take the center parts or "holes" and arrange them into a closed circle on a cookie sheet. Take a "doughnut" piece and stretch it out into a oblong. Place 1 of the narrow ends against the circle of holes to resemble the rays of the sun. Continue with the remaining pieces.

Sunrise Coffee Cake (continued)

⊙⊙

2ND RISING
Let the dough rise in a warm, draft-free spot until double: 30-45 minutes.
EGG WASH
Brush the dough with egg wash (page 21) before baking.
BAKE
Bake in oven at **375°F** for **20-25 minutes.** Cool on a wire rack immediately after baking.
ICING
When the bread has cooled, place it on a plate, fill the trays with jam and drizzle icing sugar (page 22) over all.

Stir the yeast down before adding it to the liquids in your bread bowl.

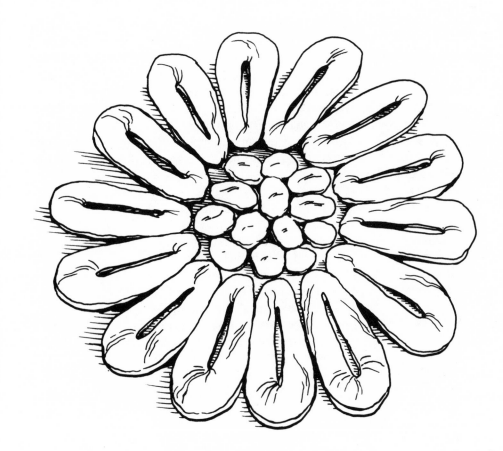

89

Finnish Coffee Braid

Makes 2 coffee cakes.

¼ **cup warm water**
1 **tsp. sugar**
2 **tbsp. yeast**
2 **eggs**
1 **cup milk, scalded**
½ **cup granulated sugar**

½ **tsp. salt**
½ **tsp. cardamom**
1 **tsp. orange peel**
½ **cup melted margarine**
4½-5 **cups flour**

PROOF
In a 1 cup measure, pour 1/4 cup warm water. Add 1 teaspoon sugar, but do not stir. Slowly sprinkle 2 tablespoons yeast into the water, making sure each particle gets wet. Again, do not stir. Wait 10 minutes until the yeast is thick and foamy.

MIX
Meanwhile, measure the following ingredients and combine them (with a wire whisk) in your bread bowl: 2 eggs, 1 cup lukewarm milk, 1/2 cup granulated sugar, 1/2 teaspoon salt, 1/2 teaspoon cardamom and 1 teaspoon orange peel. Stir the yeast down with a fork and pour it into your bread bowl. Add 1 cup of flour and stir. Add 1/2 cup cooled, melted margarine and stir.

ADD FLOUR (quickly)
You need a rather stiff dough for this recipe so that the breads will retain their shapes. Add 3½-4 cups flour, 1 cup at a time, but don't stir much between each addition. Coat the dough with flour and turn it out onto a floured kneading surface.

KNEAD
Knead gently until the dough is smooth and elastic: 10 minutes.

1ST RISING
Place the dough into a greased bowl, turn to grease the top, place in a warm, draft-free spot and allow to double in bulk: 2 hours.

SHAPE
Then punch the dough down, turn it out onto a clean surface and knead it briefly. Divide the dough in half and set it aside for 5-10 minutes.

Divide each half into 3 even pieces. Roll 3 pieces into 3 ropes, approximately 24 inches long. Braid the ropes, form into a ring, and then place on a greased baking sheet. Repeat with the 2nd half.

2ND RISING
Place in a warm, draft-free spot and allow to double in bulk: 45 minutes.

EGG WASH
Glaze the surface with an egg wash, page 21.

BAKE
Bake in a **375°F** oven for **25-30 minutes.** Cool on a wire rack, then drizzle with icing sugar glaze (page 22).

Lemon Braid

⊙⊙⊙⊙⊙⊙⊙⊙⊙⊙⊙⊙⊙⊙⊙⊙⊙⊙⊙⊙⊙⊙⊙⊙⊙⊙⊙⊙⊙⊙⊙⊙⊙⊙⊙⊙⊙⊙

Makes 2 braided loaves.

½ cup warm water	juice and peel of 1 lemon
1 tsp. sugar	nutmeg
1½ tbsp. yeast	1 cup raisins
1½ cups buttermilk, warmed	¼ cup melted butter or
2 tsp. salt	margarine
2 eggs	6 cups flour
½ cup sugar	

PROOF
In a 1 cup measure, pour 1/2 cup warm water. Add 1 teaspoon sugar, but do not stir. Slowly sprinkle 1½ tablespoons yeast into the water, making sure each particle gets wet. Again, do not stir. Wait 10 minutes until the yeast is thick and foamy.

MIX
Meanwhile mix the following in your bread bowl, stirring well between each addition: 1½ cups warm buttermilk, 2 teaspoons salt, 2 eggs, 1/2 cup sugar, juice and peel of 1 lemon, dash of nutmeg, 1 cup raisins, the yeast, 1 cup flour and 1/4 cup cooled, melted butter.

ADD FLOUR (quickly)
Add remaining flour 2 cups at a time to make a stiff dough. Make sure that the dough is coated with flour before turning it out.

KNEAD
Turn the dough out onto a lightly floured surface and knead for 10 minutes, until it is smooth and elastic.

1ST RISING
Place the dough in a greased bowl, turn to grease the top. Cover, place in a warm, draft free spot. Let rise until double: 1½ hours.

SHAPE
Cut the dough in half. Cut each half into 3 and allow them to rest for 5-10 minutes. Roll each section into a 16" long rope. Braid 3 for a loaf. Place each loaf on a greased baking sheet.

2ND RISING
Cover, place in a draft-free spot, allow to rise until double: 30-45 minutes.

EGG WASH
Gently brush with egg wash (page 21) just before baking.

BAKE
Bake in oven at **375°F** for **20-25 minutes.** Cool on wire racks immediately after baking.

GLAZE
Lemon Glaze: Mix 1 cup sifted icing sugar, 1 tsp. lemon peel and 2 tbsp. lemon juice until drizzling consistency. Add more lemon juice if too dry or more icing sugar if too wet.

Apple Raisin Twist

⊙⊙⊙

Makes 1 large or 2 smaller coffee cakes.

DOUGH:

½ **cup warm water**	3 **tbsp. sugar**
1 **tsp. sugar**	1 **tsp. salt**
1 **tbsp. yeast**	½ **cup melted butter**
½ **cup milk, scalded**	4½ **cups flour**
4 **eggs**	

PROOF

In a 1 cup measure, pour 1/2 cup warm water. Add 1 teaspoon sugar, but do not stir. Slowly sprinkle 1 tablespoon yeast into the water, making sure each particle gets wet. Again, do not stir. Wait 10 minutes until the yeast is thick and foamy.

MIX

While you are waiting, add the following ingredients to your bread bowl, stirring well between each addition: 1/2 cup warm milk, 4 eggs, 3 tablespoons sugar, 1 teaspoon salt, the yeast, 1 cup flour, 1/2 cup cooled, melted butter.

ADD FLOUR (slowly)

Add remaining flour 1 cup at a time to make a moderately soft dough. Lightly coat the dough with flour before turning it out.

KNEAD

Turn the dough out onto a lightly floured surface and knead until smooth and elastic: 8-10 minutes.

1ST RISING

Place the dough into a greased bowl, turn to grease the top, set in a warm, draft-free spot until double in bulk: 1½ hours.

Apple Raisin Twist (continued)

●○

FILLING:
melted butter
½ cup apple, peeled and
   finely chopped
2 tsp. lemon juice

1 cup raisins
½ cup brown sugar, packed
½ tsp. cinnamon

SHAPE

Punch the dough down and turn it out onto a clean surface. If you want to make 2 loaves, cut the dough in half and do the following with each half. Roll each, 1 at a time into an 8" x 12" rectangle. For 1 loaf roll the dough into a 12" x 20" rectangle. Brush the surface with melted margarine and sprinkle the filling over it. Roll the dough up like a jelly roll. Pinch the seam shut. Place the roll on a greased baking sheet (use 2 sheets for 2). Cut the roll in half, lengthwise and turn the cut side up. Gently twist the two halves together so that the filling is always exposed.

2ND RISING

Place in a warm, draft-free spot. Allow to rise until double: 30 minutes.

BAKE

350°F for **40-45 minutes** for 1 large loaf.

350°F for **30 minutes** for 2 loaves.

Note: Cover with aluminum foil after 20 minutes so that the raisins will not burn. Cool on a cake rack immediately after baking. Glaze with Icing Sugar Glaze (page 22) while still hot.

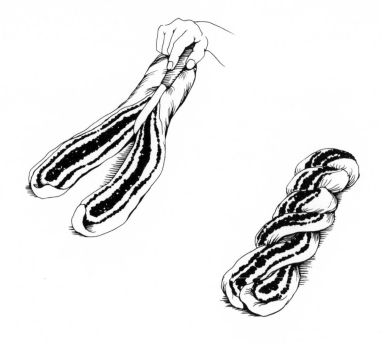

Bea's Butter Horns

An unusual recipe that is deliciously different. Serve with tea or coffee, or as a delightful dessert. These light and fluffy morsels will please the entire family.

Makes 24.

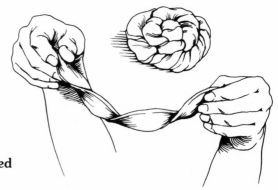

½ **cup warm water**
1 **tsp. sugar**
1 **tbsp. yeast**
⅓ **cup milk, scalded**
1 **egg, beaten**
2 **cups flour**
3 **tbsp. sugar**
⅛ **tsp. salt**
½ **cup butter, softened**

PROOF
In a 1 cup measure, pour 1/2 cup warm water. Add 1 teaspoon sugar, but do not stir. Slowly sprinkle 1 tablespoon yeast into the water, making sure each particle gets wet. Again, do not stir. Wait 10 minutes until the yeast is thick and foamy.

MIX
In a medium bowl sift together 2 cups flour, 3 tablespoons sugar, 1/8 teaspoon salt. With a pastry blender or 2 knives cut in 1/2 cup softened butter until the mixture is crumbly like pie pastry. Then add the yeast, 1/3 cup milk, 1 egg and mix just until the crumbs are moistened.

RISING
Cover the bowl and let the mixture rise overnight in the refrigerator.

SHAPE
Next morning cut the mixture in half and place 1/2 on a floured counter top. Roll with a floured rolling pin into a 12" x 15" rectangle. Cut the dough into 12-1" strips. Pick a strip up and twist it 8 times. Place it on a greased cookie sheet and wrap it into a circle. Continue with remaining dough.

BAKE
Bake in oven at **375°F** for **7-10 minutes.** Cool on a wire rack and spread with icing.

ICING
1 **tbsp. butter**
1 **cup icing sugar**
1 **tbsp. milk**

In a saucepan melt the butter and cook it until it browns. Remove from heat. Add 1 cup icing sugar and approximately 1 tablespoon milk. The icing should be of spreading consistency. If it is too wet, add more sugar. If it is too dry, add more milk.

Almond Pretzel Coffee Cake

⊙⊙⊙

Makes 1.

¼ **cup warm water**	½ **tsp. salt**
1 **tsp. sugar**	1 **tsp. lemon rind**
1 **tbsp. yeast**	1 **tsp. almond flavouring**
¼ **cup milk, scalded**	3 **tbsp. melted margarine**
⅓ **cup sour cream**	3 **cups flour**
2 **eggs**	**slivered almonds**

PROOF
In a 1 cup mesure, pour 1/4 cup warm water. Add 1 teaspoon sugar, but do not stir. Slowly sprinkle 1 tablespoon yeast into the water, making sure each particle gets wet. Again, do not stir. Wait 10 minutes until the yeast is thick and foamy.

MIX
Meanwhile add 1/4 cup warm milk, 1/3 cup sour cream, 2 eggs, 1/2 teaspoon salt, 1 teaspoon almond flavouring and 1 teaspoon lemon rind to your bread bowl. Stir well. Add the proofed yeast, 1 cup of flour and 3 tablespoons melted margarine.

ADD FLOUR (quickly)
Add remaining flour 1 cup at a time to make a stiff dough.

KNEAD
Turn out onto a lightly floured surface and knead for 8-10 minutes, until smooth and elastic.

1ST RISING
Place in a greased bowl, turn to grease the top. Place in a warm, draft-free spot until double: 1½ hours.

SHAPE
Punch dough down, turn it out, knead briefly and allow it to rest for 5 minutes. Roll it into an 18" long rope and pick up both ends with your 2 hands. Twist the dough closest to your hands 3 times then bring the ends down onto the middle of the dough. Flatten the pretzel out slightly.

2ND RISING
Place the dough on a greased baking sheet, set in a warm, draft-free spot, allow to rise until double: 30 minutes.

EGG WASH
Brush with egg wash (page 21) and sprinkle with sliced almonds.

BAKE
Bake in oven at **375°F** for **25 minutes.**

Practice makes perfect...perfectly delightful bread.

Date Nut Coffee Cake

⊙⊙⊙

You can use any filling for this pretty bread, simply make sure that it is thick and will not run while baking.

Makes 2 coffee cakes.

FILLING:

1½ **cups pitted dates,**   1 **cup water**
      chopped   ¾ **cup chopped nuts**
⅓ **cup brown sugar**   1½ **tablespoons lemon juice**

Combine the filling ingredients in a saucepan and bring to a boil. Boil until thick and of spreading consistency. Remove from heat and cool.

DOUGH:

½ **cup warm water**   1½ **tsp. salt**
1 **tsp. sugar**   2 **eggs**
2 **tbsp. yeast**   4-4½ **cups flour**
¼ **cup milk, scalded**   ¼ **cup melted shortening**
¼ **cup sugar**

PROOF
In a 1 cup measure, pour 1/2 cup warm water. Add 1 teaspoon sugar, but do not stir. Slowly sprinkle 2 tablespoons yeast into the water, making sure each particle gets wet. Again, do not stir. Wait 10 minutes until the yeast is thick and foamy.

MIX
While you are waiting, add the following ingredients to your bread bowl, stirring well between each addition: 1/4 cup warm milk, 1/4 cup sugar, 1½ teaspoons salt, 2 eggs, the proofed yeast, 1 cup flour, 1/4 cup cooled, melted shortening.

ADD FLOUR (quickly)
Add remaining flour 1 cup at a time to make a stiff dough. Lightly coat the dough with flour before turning it out.

KNEAD
Turn the dough out onto a lightly floured surface and knead until smooth and elastic: 8-10 minutes.

1ST RISING:
Place the dough in a greased bowl, turn to grease the top, set in a warm, draft-free spot until double: 1½ hours.

Date Nut Coffee Cake (continued)

ⓞⓞⓞⓞⓞⓞⓞⓞⓞⓞⓞⓞⓞⓞⓞⓞⓞⓞⓞⓞⓞⓞⓞⓞⓞⓞⓞⓞⓞⓞⓞⓞⓞⓞⓞⓞⓞⓞⓞ

SHAPE

When the dough has doubled punch it down and turn it out onto a clean surface. Knead briefly and shape into a smooth ball. Cut the dough in half and roll 1/2 on a lightly floured surface into a 16" x 8" rectangle. Turn and flour the dough a few times while rolling so that it will not stick to the counter. Spread the cooled filling down the middle third of the dough. Cut 15- 1" slits on either side of the filling. Make sure that the slits are of even length and width for an attractive loaf. Alternating sides, fold one strip across the filling and cover it with the opposite strip. Place on a greased baking sheet. Do the same with the other half.

2ND RISING

Place the dough in a warm, draft-free spot, allow to rise until double: 30 minutes.

EGG WASH

Brush with egg wash (page 21) before baking.

BAKE

Bake in oven at **375°F** for **35 minutes.** Cool immediately after baking on a wire rack.

GLAZE

Drizzle with Icing Sugar Glaze (page 22) while still warm.

Cover the dough with a tea towel if you are not using fool-proof proofing.

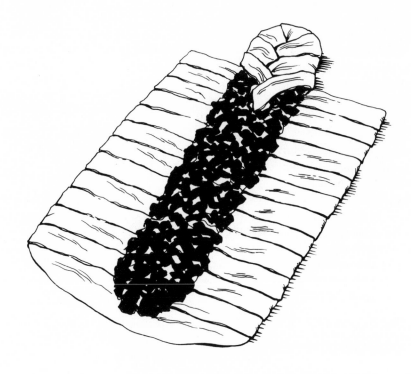

Coffee Breakers

🔘🔘🔘🔘🔘🔘🔘🔘🔘🔘🔘🔘🔘🔘🔘🔘🔘🔘🔘🔘🔘🔘🔘🔘🔘🔘🔘🔘🔘🔘🔘

Makes 48 buns.

TOPPING:
1 **cup brown sugar**
3 **tbsp. corn syrup**
½ **cup melted margarine**
1 **cup pecans or walnuts,**
   chopped

Combine the topping ingredients in a saucepan and bring to a boil. Spread topping on 2 jelly roll pans. Sprinkle with chopped pecans or walnuts.

DOUGH:
1 **cup warm water**
1 **tsp. sugar**
3 **tbsp. yeast**
2 **cups milk, scalded**
½ **cup melted margarine,**
   cooled
1 **cup sugar**
1 **tbsp. salt**
4 **eggs**
9-10 **cups flour**

PROOF
In a 2 cup measure, pour 1 cup warm water. Add 1 teaspoon sugar, but do not stir. Slowly sprinkle 3 tablespoons yeast into the water, making sure each particle gets wet. Again, do not stir. Wait 10 minutes until the yeast is thick and foamy.

MIX
Meanwhile, pour the 2 cups warm milk into your bread bowl. Add 1 cup sugar, 1 tablespoon salt and 4 eggs. Beat this mixture until smooth with a wire whisk. Add the proofed yeast and stir in 2 cups of flour. Beat until smooth. Add 1/2 cup margarine, stir.

ADD FLOUR (slowly)
Add remaining flour to make a soft dough. When the dough is of the desired consistency, clean it away from the sides of the bowl, coat it lightly with flour and turn it out onto a floured kneading surface.

Coffee Breakers (continued)

⊙⊙⊙

KNEAD
Gently knead for 10 minutes, until the dough is smooth and elastic.
1ST RISING
Place the dough in a greased bowl, turn to grease the top, set in a warm, draft-free spot and allow to rise until double in bulk: 1½-2 hours.
SHAPE
When the dough has doubled punch it down and turn it out onto the kneading surface. Knead it briefly into a neat ball and cut it into 4 pieces. Work with 1 piece at a time.

FILLING:
1 **cup brown sugar**
1-2 **tbsp. cinnamon**
melted margarine

SHAPE
Roll 1 piece out into a 12" square. Brush the entire surface with melted margarine. Sprinkle the center 1/3 with 2 tablespoons of the filling. Fold 1/3 of the dough over filling, brush with margarine, and sprinkle it with 2 table-spoons of filling. Cover the filling with the remaining third. Cut the long narrow strip (12" x 3") into 1" pieces. Twist each piece 3 times and place on cookie sheet. Continue this process with the remaining quarters.
2ND RISING
Set in a warm, draft-free spot and allow to rise until double: 20-30 minutes.
BAKE
Bake in a **400°F** oven for **15-20 minutes.** When baked turn the buns out onto cooling racks, topping side up.

The Three Bears

⊙⊙

A whole wheat treat for the sweet tooth. These bears will make you a big hit with your children. Try it, they'll love it!

$\frac{1}{2}$ **cup warm water**
1 **tsp. sugar**
2 **tbsp. yeast**
1$\frac{3}{4}$ **cup milk, scalded**
2 **eggs**
1$\frac{1}{2}$ **tsp. salt**
1 **cup sugar OR**
$\frac{1}{2}$ **cup honey**
1 **cup melted margarine**
4 **cups whole wheat flour**
3$\frac{1}{2}$-4 **cups flour**
1 **egg, beaten**

PROOF
In a 1 cup measure, pour 1/2 cup warm water. Add 1 teaspoon sugar, but do not stir. Slowly sprinkle 2 tablespoons yeast into the water, making sure each particle gets wet. Again, do not stir. Wait 10 minutes until the yeast is thick and foamy.

MIX
Meanwhile mix the following ingredients together in your bread bowl, stirring well between each addition: 1$\frac{3}{4}$ cup warm milk, 2 eggs, 1$\frac{1}{2}$ teaspoons salt and 1 cup sugar. Add the yeast and 1 cup of whole wheat flour. Add the cooled, melted margarine and stir.

ADD FLOUR (slowly)
First add the remaining whole wheat flour, 1 cup at a time, then the white flour, 1 cup at a time. Make sure that the dough has a light coating of flour before turning it out.

KNEAD
Turn the dough out onto a lightly floured surface and knead for 12 minutes, until elastic.

1ST RISING
Place the dough in a greased bowl, turn to grease the top, place in a warm, draft-free place, allow to rise until double in bulk: 1$\frac{1}{2}$ hours.

The Three Bears (continued)

SHAPE

Punch the dough down and turn it out onto a clean surface. Cut the dough into 3 pieces making sure that 1 piece is slightly larger than the other so that you can have the 3 bears.

Do the same with each piece:

Cut 1 piece in half and shape 1/2 into a ball. Place it on a cookie sheet and flatten it a bit. This is the body of the bear. As you attach the remaining pieces remember to brush them with some of the beaten egg and tuck them under the body. Don't get any egg on the cookie sheet or it will stick after baking. Cut the remaining half in half and shape 1/2 into a ball for the head. Place it slightly under the body. Roll the dough that's left into a 7" rope. Use 2" for the snout, pinching a bit off for the nose. Use 2-1/2" pieces for the ears and 4- 1" pieces for the legs. Repeat with Mama and baby bear.

2ND RISING

Place the bears in a warm, draft-free spot and let them rise until double: 30 minutes.

EGG WASH

Brush the bears with egg wash (page 21) just before baking.
has been added.

BAKE

Bake in oven at **375°F** for **30 minutes**. Immediately after baking cool the bears on a wire rack. Be careful when handling the bears that they don't fall apart. If you do find that the bears fall apart its because you either did not use enough egg or did not tuck the pieces under the body well enough.

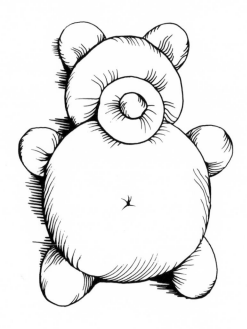

Filled Apple Kuchen

☉☉

Picture yourself on a crisp fall day, sitting in front of a crackling fire, with a steaming cup of coffee, and a plate full of kuchen, fresh out of the oven — superb! This recipe is similar to Bea's Butter Horns because the dough is like pie pastry.

Serves 6.

¼ **cup warm water**	1 **tsp. vanilla**
1 **tsp. sugar**	2 **lbs. peeled and sliced**
1 **tbsp. yeast**	**apples (Spies or**
2 **cups flour**	**MacIntosh)**
½ **tsp. salt**	1-1½ **cups sugar**
2 **tbsp. sugar**	2 **tbsp. flour**
1 **cup shortening**	¼ **cup butter**
1 **egg**	**cinnamon, to taste**

PROOF

In a 1 cup measure, pour 1/4 cup warm water. Add 1 teaspoon sugar, but do not stir. Slowly sprinkle 1 tablespoon yeast into the water, making sure each particle gets wet. Again, do not stir. Wait 10 minutes until the yeast is thick and foamy.

MIX

Meanwhile, sift 2 cups flour, 1/2 teaspoon salt and 2 tablespoons sugar together. Mix 1 cup shortening into the flour with a pastry blender or 2 knives, until the dough is the size of peas. With a wooden spoon stir in the proofed yeast, 1 egg and 1 teaspoon vanilla. Coat the dough with flour.

KNEAD

Turn the dough out onto a lightly floured surface and knead for 2 minutes. By then the dough should be similar to pastry, not sticky or gummy.

Filled Apple Kuchen

⊙⊙

SHAPE

Cut the dough into 2 pieces making 1 piece slightly larger than the other. Grease a 10" x 14" (or larger) jelly roll pan or good quality cookie sheet, and set it aside. Now, roll the larger half of the dough on a floured surface into a very thin 11" x 15" rectangle. Keep flouring the underside of the dough to prevent it from sticking. Place the dough in the pan making sure that the dough overlaps the sides of the pan. Arrange the apples evenly over the dough. Sprinkle 2 tablespoons flour, from 1-1½ cups sugar (depending on tartness of the apples) and cinnamon over the apples. Dot with 1/4 cup butter and set aside.

Roll the smaller piece of dough into a 10" x 14" rectangle. Place it over the apples and seal the edges with the overlapping dough. Prick the top with a fork, brush it with milk, and sprinkle with 2 tablespoons sugar and cinnamon to taste.

BAKE

Don't let the dough rise, bake it immediately after shaping. Bake in a **325°F** oven for **30-50 minutes,** depending on the apples. Be careful that it does not brown too much. Serve warm.

Always read the recipe before starting.

Chelsea Buns

Makes 1- 8½" x 12" pan or 2- 8" x 8" pan.

TOPPING:

¼ cup margarine

¾ cup brown sugar

3 tbsp. corn syrup

¾ cup chopped nuts

Melt these ingredients together in a saucepan and quickly spread it into your choice of the above pans. Set aside.

DOUGH:

½ cup warm water

2 tbsp. yeast

1 tsp. sugar

1 cup milk, scalded

½ cup granulated sugar

¼ cup margarine

2 tsp. salt

1 egg

5 cups flour

PROOF

In a 1 cup measure, pour 1/2 cup warm water. Add 1 teaspoon sugar, but do not stir. Slowly sprinkle 2 tablespoons yeast into the water, making sure each particle gets wet. Again, do not stir. Wait 10 minutes until the yeast is thick and foamy.

MIX

Meanwhile add the following ingredients to your bread bowl, stirring well between each addition: 1 cup warm milk, 1/2 cup sugar, 2 teaspoons salt and 1 egg. When the yeast is light and spongy add it to the ingredients already in your bread bowl. Stir in 1 cup of flour, then add 1/4 cup warm, melted margarine.

ADD FLOUR (slowly)

Add the remaining flour 1 cup at a time to get a soft dough.

KNEAD

Turn out onto a lightly floured kneading surface and knead until smooth and elastic: 10 minutes.

SHAPE

Then roll the dough out into a 12" x 18" rectangle.

FILLING:

½ cup brown sugar

¼ cup chopped nuts

½ cup raisins

cinnamon

Brush the dough with melted margarine, then spread brown sugar over the dough with the back of a spoon. Sprinkle the surface with cinnamon, chopped nuts and raisins.

Roll the dough up like a jelly roll. Cut into 18 pieces for 2- 8" x 8" pans or 12 pieces for 1- 8½" x 12" pan. Arrange, cut side up, on top of topping. Set in a warm, draft-free spot and allow to rise until double: 30-45 minutes.

BAKE

Bake in a **375°F** oven for **25 minutes**. Remove from oven and allow to cool for 30 seconds, then turn them out onto a cake rack to cool.

Baked Doughnuts

⊙⊙⊙⊙⊙⊙⊙⊙⊙⊙⊙⊙⊙⊙⊙⊙⊙⊙⊙⊙⊙⊙⊙⊙⊙⊙⊙⊙⊙⊙⊙⊙⊙⊙⊙⊙⊙

- 1 **tbsp. yeast**
- ¼ **cup warm potato water**
- 1 **cup mashed potatoes**
- 1 **cup milk**
- ¾ **cup shortening**
- ½ **cup sugar**
- 1 **tsp. salt**
- 2 **eggs, well beaten**
- 4½ **cups flour**

PROOF

In a 1 cup measure, pour 1/4 cup warm potato water. Slowly sprinkle 1 tablespoon yeast into the water, making sure each particle gets wet. Do not stir. Wait 10 minutes until the yeast is thick and foamy.

MIX

In a saucepan add 1 cup milk, 3/4 cup shortening, 1/2 cup sugar and 1 tsp. salt. Place over medium heat until the shortening melts. Add 1 cup potatoes. Pour the shortening mixture into your bread bowl and allow to cool. Stir in the proofed yeast and 2 beaten eggs. Add 4½ cups flour, 1 cup at a time.

1ST RISING

Scrape down the sides of the bowl, cover, let rise until light: 1 hour.

KNEAD

Turn out onto a lightly floured board and knead until smooth: 8 minutes. The shortening makes this dough feel light and it will not stick to your hands or the kneading surface.

SHAPE

Roll the dough with a rolling pin to a 1/2 inch thickness. Wait a minute, then cut with a doughnut cutter. You will find that the longer you wait before you cut the doughnuts out the better they will look. Keep gathering the dough up and rolling it out to make more doughnuts.

2ND RISING

Place doughnuts on a greased baking sheet, set in a warm, draft-free spot and allow to rise until double: 30 minutes

BAKE

Bake in a **400°F** oven for **10-15 minutes.**

TOPPINGS:

Butter all sides and dip into either white or cinnamon sugar.

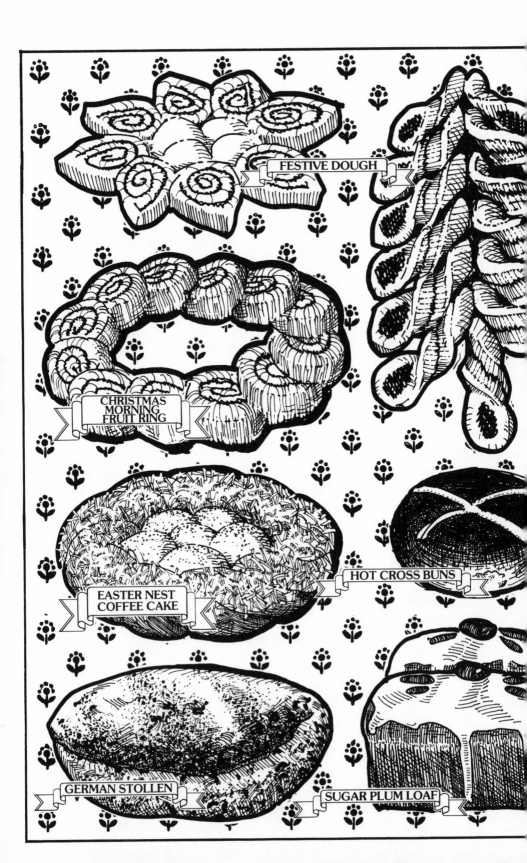

FESTIVE DOUGH

CHRISTMAS
MORNING
FRUIT RING

EASTER NEST
COFFEE CAKE

HOT CROSS BUNS

GERMAN STOLLEN

SUGAR PLUM LOAF

FESTIVE BREAD

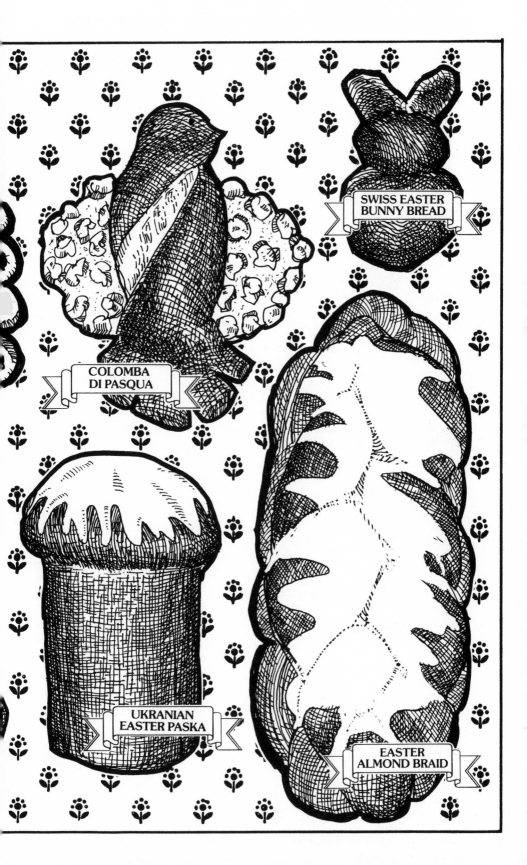

SWISS EASTER
BUNNY BREAD

COLOMBA
DI PASQUA

UKRANIAN
EASTER PASKA

EASTER
ALMOND BRAID

Easter Nest Coffee Cake

◉◉

Makes 1.

- 1 **tbsp. yeast**
- ¼ **cup water**
- 1 **tsp. sugar**
- ½ **cup milk, scalded**
- ¼ **cup sugar**
- ¼ **cup melted margarine**
- 1 **tsp. salt**
- 3-3½ **cups flour**
- 1 **egg**
- **coconut**
- **green food colouring**
- **confectioner's icing**
- **decorations**

PROOF

In a 1 cup measure, pour 1/4 cup warm water. Add 1 teaspoon sugar, but do not stir. Slowly sprinkle 1 tablespoon yeast into the water, making sure each particle gets wet. Again, do not stir. Wait 10 minutes until the yeast is thick and foamy.

MIX

Meanwhile, in your bread bowl add the following ingredients, stirring well between each addition: 1/2 cup warm milk, 1/4 cup sugar, 1 egg and 1 teaspoon salt. Add proofed yeast and 1 cup flour. Then add 1/4 cup cooled, melted margarine.

ADD FLOUR (quickly)

Add remaining flour to make a moderately stiff dough. Lightly coat the dough with flour before turning it out.

KNEAD

Turn out onto a lightly floured surface and knead until smooth and elastic: 8 minutes.

1ST RISING

Place in a greased bowl, turn to grease the top, set in a warm, draft-free spot and allow to rise until double: 1½ hours.

Easter Nest Coffee Cake (continued)

SHAPE
Punch down, divide into thirds and allow to rest. Shape 1/3 of the dough into 6 eggs and place close together in the center of a greased baking sheet. For the nest, shape remaining dough into 2- 26" ropes; twist together. Coil around the eggs. Seal the ends.

2ND RISING
Cover and set in a warm, draft-free spot to rise until double in bulk: 30 minutes.

EGG WASH
Brush with egg wash (page 21) just before baking.

BAKE
Bake in a **375°F** oven for **15-20 minutes.** Cool on a rack. Tint the coconut with green food colouring. Now spread Icing Sugar Glaze (page 22) over the warm cake. Sprinkle the coconut on the braided part of the nest and decorate the eggs with candy sprinkles.

Hot Cross Buns

Makes 12-16 buns.

½ **cup warm water**	2½ **tsp. cinnamon**
1 **tbsp. yeast**	¾ **tsp. cloves**
1 **tsp. sugar**	¼ **tsp. nutmeg**
¾ **cup milk, scalded**	1 **cup raisins**
2 **eggs**	½ **cup currants (or peel)**
½ **cup sugar**	¼ **cup melted margarine**
1 **tsp. salt**	4½-5 **cups flour**

PROOF

In a 1 cup measure, pour 1/2 cup warm water. Add 1 teaspoon sugar, but do not stir. Slowly sprinkle 1 tablespoon yeast into the water, making sure each particle gets wet. Again, do not stir. Wait 10 minutes until the yeast is thick and foamy.

MIX

Meanwhile, in your bread bowl, add the following ingredients, stirring well between each addition: 3/4 cup cooled milk, 2 eggs, 1/2 cup sugar, 1 teaspoon salt, 2½ teaspoons cinnamon, 3/4 teaspoon cloves, 1/4 teaspoon nutmeg, the yeast, 1 cup raisins, 1/2 cup currants, 1 cup flour and 1/4 cup cooled margarine.

ADD FLOUR (quickly)

Add remaining flour 1 cup at a time to make a fairly stiff dough. Coat the dough lightly with flour before turning it out.

KNEAD

Turn the dough out onto a lightly floured surface and knead until smooth and elastic: 10 minutes.

1ST RISING

Place the dough in a greased bowl, turn to grease the top, set in a warm, draft-free spot until double: 1½ hours.

SHAPE

Punch the dough down and turn it out onto a clean surface. Roll it into a 12"-16" rope, depending on how many buns you want to make. Cut the rope into 12-16 pieces and shape each into a smooth ball. Place each ball on a greased cookie sheet. Flatten each one slightly.

2ND RISING

Set cookie sheets in a warm, draft-free spot until double: 30-45 minutes.

EGG WASH

Brush with egg wash (page 21) just before baking.

BAKE

Bake at 375°F in oven for **15-18 minutes.** Cool immediately on a wire rack.

GLAZE

Make Icing Sugar Glaze and drizzle crosses on the buns (page 22).

If your dough over rises during 2nd Rising, punch it down, reshape it, and let it rise again.

Easter Almond Braid

⊙⊙⊙

Makes 2.

> 2 **tbsp. yeast**
> ½ **cup warm water**
> 1 **tsp. sugar**
> 1 **cup milk, scalded**
> ½ **cup melted margarine**
> ½ **cup sugar**
> 1½ **tsp. salt**
> 2 **eggs**
> 1 **tsp. vanilla or**
> **almond extract**
> 5-5½ **cups flour**
> 5-7 **tbsp. almond paste**

PROOF
In a 1 cup measure, pour 1/2 cup warm water. Add 1 teaspoon sugar, but do not stir. Slowly sprinkle 2 tablespoons yeast into the water, making sure each particle gets wet. Again, do not stir. Wait 10 minutes until the yeast is thick and foamy.

MIX
Meanwhile, in a bread bowl combine the following ingredients, stirring well between each addition: 1 cup warm milk, 1/2 cup sugar, 1½ teaspoons salt, 2 eggs, 1 teaspoon flavouring and 1 cup of the flour. Stir down yeast and add to mixture. Add 1/2 cup cooled, melted margarine.

ADD FLOUR (quickly)
Add remaining flour 1 cup at a time to make a stiff dough.

KNEAD
Turn out onto a lightly floured surface and knead until smooth and elastic: 10 minutes. Place dough in a greased bowl, turn to grease the top and set in a warm, draft-free spot, allow to rise until double: 1½ hours.

SHAPE
Punch down, cut in half and allow to rest. Divide first half into 1/3 and 2/3. Divide larger piece in 3 and roll out into 16" ropes. Braid. With the side of your hand make a trench down the center of the braid. Fill with half the almond paste. Make a smaller braid out of the remaining piece and place it on top. Spread lightly with almond paste. Do the same with the other half and allow to rise until double: 30 minutes.

EGG WASH
Brush with egg wash, page 21.

BAKE
Bake in a **325°F** oven for **45-50 minutes.** Cool on a wire rack.

Swiss Easter Bunny Bread

ⓄⓄ

Makes 6-10 bunnies.

2 **tbsp. yeast**	2 **tbsp. sugar**
½ **cup warm water**	1 **tsp. salt**
1 **tsp. sugar**	5-5½ **cups flour**
1¼ **cup milk, scalded**	1 **egg**
½ **cup &** 3 **tbsp. margarine**	**currants or raisins**

PROOF

In a 1 cup measure, pour 1/2 cup warm water. Add 1 teaspoon sugar, but do not stir. Slowly sprinkle 2 tablespoons yeast into the water, making sure each particle gets wet. Again, do not stir. Wait 10 minutes until the yeast is thick and foamy.

MIX

Meanwhile, in a bread bowl add the following ingredients, stirring well between each addition: 1¼ cup warm milk, 2 tablespoons sugar, 1 teaspoon salt and 1 egg. Stir in yeast and 1 cup flour. Add 1/2 cup and 3 tablespoons margarine, cooled.

ADD FLOUR (slowly)

Add remaining flour to make a moderately soft dough. Coat the dough lightly with flour before turning it out.

KNEAD

Knead until smooth and elastic: 10 minutes.

1ST RISING

Place in a greased bowl, turn to grease the top, set in a warm, draft-free spot and allow to rise until double in bulk: 1½ hours.

SHAPE

Punch down, turn out and allow to rest for 10 minutes. Depending on the size bunny you want, divide the dough into between 6 to 10 pieces. For each bunny you will need 1 large and 2 smaller balls of dough. Place large ball (body) and 1 smaller ball (head) on greased baking sheet. Flatten down. Stretch third ball lengthwise and press onto top of head. With scissors, make deep slash down center to form ears; spread apart.

2ND RISING

Cover and allow to rise in a warm, draft-free spot until double: 30 minutes

EGG WASH

Brush with egg wash, page 21.

BAKE

Bake in **350°F** oven for **20-30 minutes** depending on size. You can make a whole family of bunnies. Decorate *after* baking, using currants or raisins for eyes.

Ukrainian Easter Paska

1½ **tbsp. yeast**	1 **tsp. lemon peel**
½ **cup warm water**	1½ **tsp. vanilla**
1 **tsp. sugar**	½ **tsp. salt**
½ **cup milk, scalded**	½ **cup melted margarine**
3 **eggs**	4-4½ **cups flour**
1 **cup sugar**	**lemon glaze**

PROOF

In a 1 cup measure, pour 1/2 cup warm water. Add 1 teaspoon sugar, but do not stir. Slowly sprinkle 1½ tablespoons yeast into the water, making sure each particle gets wet. Again, do not stir. Wait 10 minutes until the yeast is thick and foamy.

MIX

Add the following ingredients to your bread bowl, stirring well between each addition: 1/2 cup warm milk, 3 eggs, 1 cup sugar, 1 teaspoon lemon peel, 1½ teaspoons vanilla, 1/2 teaspoon salt, the proofed yeast, 1 cup flour and 1/2 cup cooled margarine.

ADD FLOUR (slowly)

Add the remaining flour, 1 cup at a time to make a soft dough. Coat the dough lightly with flour before turning it out.

KNEAD

Turn the dough out onto a lightly floured surface and knead until smooth and elastic: 8 minutes.

1ST RISING

Place the dough in a greased bowl, turn to grease the top, set in a warm, draft-free spot, allow to rise until double: 1½ hours.

SHAPE

When the dough has doubled turn it out onto a clean surface and knead for 1 minute. The number of loaves you make depends on the size of can that you use. A 3 pound shortening can makes 2 loaves, coffee cans make 3 loaves, etc. The best rule to follow is to use enough dough to fill the can only 1/2 full. If you use too much dough it will fall over the sides of the can and will be impossible to get out after baked. Also it will be top-heavy so that it will not stand upright after baking. Make sure the can you use has straight sides, if not the bread will not come out after baking. So cut the dough into the desired number of pieces, smooth each piece out and place it into a well greased can to fill the can only 1/2 full.

2ND RISING

Set the cans in a warm, draft-free spot, allow to rise until double: 30 minutes.

BAKE

Set your oven rack so that the dough will not touch the roof of your oven. Bake in a **325°F** oven for **50-60 minutes** until the loaf comes out of the can easily. Cool horizontally on a wire rack. Drizzle Lemon Glaze (page 91) down the sides and decorate with candy sprinkles.

113

Colomba Di Pasqua

Makes 2.

- 1 **tbsp. yeast**
- ¼ **cup warm water**
- 1 **tsp. sugar**
- ½ **cup melted margarine**
- ½ **cup plus 2 tbsp. sugar**
- 1 **tsp. lemon peel**
- 2 **tsp. vanilla**
- ½ **tsp. salt**
- 4 **eggs**
- ½ **cup milk, scalded**
- 5-5½ **cups flour**
- 5 **tbsp. almond paste**
  blanched almonds

PROOF

In a 1 cup measure, pour 1/4 cup warm water. Add 1 teaspoon sugar, but do not stir. Slowly sprinkle 1 tablespoon yeast into the water, making sure each particle gets wet. Again, do not stir. Wait 10 minutes until the yeast is thick and foamy.

MIX

Meanwhile, in bread bowl measure out 1/2 cup of sugar, 1 teaspoon lemon peel, 2 teaspoon vanilla, 1/2 teaspoon salt, 4 eggs, 1/2 cup milk and 1 cup flour. Add yeast and stir until smooth with wire whisk. Add 1/2 cup cooled, melted margarine.

ADD FLOUR (quickly)

Add remaining flour 1 cup at a time to get a moderately stiff dough. Lightly coat the dough with flour before turning it out.

KNEAD

Turn out onto a lightly floured surface and knead until smooth and elastic: 10 minutes.

1ST RISING

Place in a greased bowl, turn to grease the top, set in a warm, draft-free spot and allow to rise until double: 1½ hours.

Colomba Di Pasqua (continued)

SHAPE
Punch down and divide in half and allow to rest. Cut each half into 1/2 and shape into smooth balls. Roll out first ball into a long oval for wings. Roll out second into a triangle and place over wings. Twist narrow end of triangle one way to form the head; pull at the end to shape a beak. Twist wide end of triangle in opposite direction to form tail. Slash base of tail to resemble feathers. Spread with almond paste and sprinkle with remaining 2 tablespoons sugar.

2ND RISING
Set in a warm, draft-free spot and let rise until double: 30 minutes.

EGG WASH
Brush dove with egg wash, page 21. Sprinkle tail and wings with sugar and sliced almonds.

BAKE
Bake at **350°F** for **30-35 minutes** or until golden brown. Cool immediately on a wire rack.

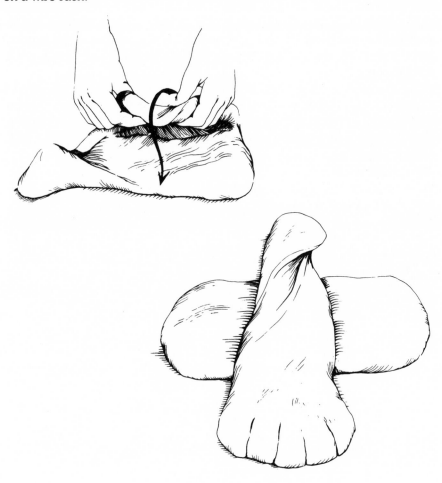

Festive Dough

2 tbsp. yeast
1¼ cup warm water
1 tsp. sugar
⅓ cup skim milk powder
½ cup sugar
2 tsp. salt
2 eggs
1 tsp. lemon peel
¼ cup melted margarine
4½-5 cups flour

PROOF

In a bread bowl, pour 1¼ cups warm water. Add 1 teaspoon sugar, but do not stir. Slowly sprinkle 2 tablespoons yeast into the water, making sure each particle gets wet. Again, do not stir. Wait 10 minutes until the yeast is thick and foamy.

MIX

Then add 1/3 cup skim milk powder, 1/2 cup sugar, 2 teaspoons salt, 2 eggs, 1 teaspoon lemon peel and 1 cup of flour. Whisk these ingredients together until the dough is smooth. Add 1/4 cup cooled margarine. Whisk again.

ADD FLOUR (quickly)

Add the remaining flour, 1 cup at a time, to make a moderately stiff dough. Coat the dough with flour.

KNEAD

Turn the dough out onto a lightly floured kneading surface. Knead until smooth and elastic: 10 minutes.

1ST RISING

Place the dough into a greased bowl, turn to grease the top, cover and allow to rise until double: 1½ hours.

Festive Dough (continued)

SHAPE

Punch the dough down, turn it out and knead to remove all the large bubbles. Let it rest for 10 minutes then form into desired shape:

Christmas Trees: Divide the dough into thirds. For each tree roll one third into a 12" x 6" rectangle. Spread with 1 tablespoon melted butter; sprinkle with 1 tablespoon red or green sugar crystals. Fold in half to make a 12" x 3" rectangle. Cut into 12- 1" strips. Twist each one 3 times and arrange on a greased baking sheet with the loose ends in the center. Use 10 strips for branches and 1 strip for the base. Cut the remaining strip in half; use as top branches for the tree. Place in a warm, draft-free spot until doubled: 30 minutes.

Poinsettias: Divide dough in half. Roll each into a 16" x 12" rectangle. Brush with melted butter. Mix 1/2 cup finely chopped glace cherries and 3 tablespoons sugar; sprinkle over the dough. Roll it up like a jelly roll, seal edge. Cut the roll into 12 equal pieces. Reserve the 2 end pieces for the center. Place remaining slices, cut side down, on a greased baking sheet. Arrange in a circle around a 2" center space with each slice overlapping slightly.

Pinch outside edges of each slice to make petal tip. Divide each end piece in half; shape into balls. Place balls in center. Repeat with second half of dough. Place in a warm, draft-free spot until doubled: 30 minutes.

EGG WASH

Before baking brush the dough with an egg wash, page 21.

BAKE

Bake in a **375°F** oven for approximately **20 minutes,** keeping a close watch that they do not overcook. Cool on a wire rack. Ice with Icing Sugar Glaze page 22.

Sugar Plum Loaf

Makes 6 small loaves.

1 **cup warm water**
1 **tsp. sugar**
2 **tbsp. yeast**
1 **tsp. salt**
2 **eggs**
½ **cup sugar**
⅓ **cup skim milk powder**
1 **cup chopped walnuts**

¼ **cup candied cherries, chopped**
¼ **cup candied pineapple, chopped**
1 **tsp. cardamom**
¼ **cup melted margarine**
4 **cups flour**

PROOF

In a bread bowl, pour 1 cup warm water. Add 1 teaspoon sugar, but do not stir. Slowly sprinkle 2 tablespoons yeast into the water, making sure each particle gets wet. Again, do not stir. Wait 10 minutes until the yeast is thick and foamy.

MIX

Then add the following ingredients, stirring well between each addition: 1 teaspoon salt, 2 eggs, 1/2 cup sugar, 1/3 cup skim milk powder, 1 cup walnuts, 1/4 cup candied cherries, 1/4 cup candied pineapple, 1 teaspoon cardamom, 1 cup flour and 1/4 cup cooled margarine.

ADD FLOUR (slowly)

This dough is unusual to work with because of all the fruit in it. Add the remaining flour slowly so that you incorporate all of it into the dough, the dough may seem stiff. Coat the dough lightly with flour before turning it out.

KNEAD

Turn the dough out onto a lightly floured surface and knead until elastic: 10 minutes. This is a sticky one so be patient.

1ST RISING

Place the dough in a greased bowl, turn to grease the top, set in a warm place until double in bulk: 2 hours.

SHAPE

Punch the dough down and turn it out onto a clean surface. Cut the dough into 6 pieces and shape each into a smooth ball. You can either bake the dough as it is on a greased baking sheet, or place them in greased loaf tins. You can buy little foil tins that are just the right size (4¼" x 3¼" x 1¾" deep) and there are 6 in a package..

2ND RISE

Set the loaves in a warm, draft-free spot and allow to rise until doubled: 1 hour.

EGG WASH

Just before baking brush the loaves with egg wash (page 21).

BAKE

Bake in a **375°F** oven for **20-25 minutes**. Cool immediately after baking on a wire rack. Decorate with Icing Sugar Glaze page 22.

German Stollen

⊙⊙⊙

Makes 2.

½ **cup raisins**
¼ **cup currants**
½ **cup chopped candied fruit
    (green and red cherries,
    pineapple, peel)**
¼ **cup rum**

Soak fruit in rum.

2 **tbsp. yeast**	¼ **cup sugar**
1 **cup warm water**	2 **eggs**
1 **tsp. sugar**	½ **tsp. almond extract**
⅓ **cup skim milk powder**	2 **tsp. grated orange peel**
½ **cup melted margarine**	1 **tsp. lemon peel**
1 **tsp. salt**	4-4½ **cups flour**

PROOF
In a bread bowl, pour 1 cup warm water. Add 1 teaspoon sugar, but do not stir. Slowly sprinkle 2 tablespoons yeast into the water, making sure each particle gets wet. Again, do not stir. Wait 10 minutes until the yeast is thick and foamy.

MIX
Then add 1 cup of flour to proofed yeast and beat well with 1/3 cup skim milk powder, 1/2 cup cooled margarine, 1 teaspoon salt, 1/4 cup sugar, 2 eggs, 1/2 teaspoon almond extract, 1 teaspoon lemon and 2 teaspoons orange peel and 1 more cup flour. Stir in candied fruit. Add remaining flour, 1 cup at a time to retain a soft dough. Coat dough with flour, turn out onto a floured kneading surface.

KNEAD
Knead lightly for 10 minutes until smooth and elastic.

1ST RISING
Place dough in a greased bowl, turn to grease the top. Set in a warm, draft-free spot and allow to rise until double: 1½ hours.

SHAPE
Punch dough down, knead briefly, divide in half, cover and allow to rest for 10 minutes. Roll each half into a 10" x 7" oval. Fold long side of oval over to within 1/2" of the opposite side; seal edge. Place on greased baking sheet, and set in a warm, draft-free spot to rise until double: 30 minutes.

BAKE
Bake in a **375°F** oven for **20 minutes**. Dust with icing sugar. Decorate with candied fruit.

Christmas Morning Fruit Ring

Serve for your Christmas brunch or enjoy it while opening gifts.

DOUGH:
1 **cup warm water**
1 **tsp. sugar**
1 **tbsp. yeast**
½ **cup milk, scalded**
2 **eggs**
½ **cup sugar**
½ **tsp. salt**
¼ **cup melted margarine**
5 **cups flour**

FILLING:
¼ **cup melted butter**
½ **tsp. cinnamon**
¼ **cup currants**
¼ **cup lemon peel**
¼ **cup candied cherries,**
　　chopped

PROOF

In a 2 cup measure, pour 1 cup warm water. Add 1 teaspoon sugar, but do not stir. Slowly sprinkle 1 tablespoon yeast into the water, making sure each particle gets wet. Again, do not stir. Wait 10 minutes until the yeast is thick and foamy.

MIX

While you are waiting for the yeast to proof mix the following ingredients in your bread bowl, stirring well between each addition: 1/2 cup warm milk, 2 eggs, 1/2 cup sugar, 1/2 teaspoon salt, the proofed yeast, 1 cup flour and 1/4 cup cooled margarine.

ADD FLOUR (quickly)

Add remaining flour 1 cup at a time to make a stiff dough. Lightly coat the dough with flour before turning it out.

KNEAD

Turn the dough out onto a floured surface and knead until smooth and elastic: 10 minutes.

Christmas Morning Fruit Ring
(continued)

⊙⊙

1ST RISING
Place the dough in a greased bowl, turn to grease the top, set in a warm, draft-free spot until double in bulk: 1½-2 hours.

SHAPE
Punch the dough down and turn it out onto a lightly floured surface. Cut the dough in half and work with 1/2 at a time. Roll 1/2 into a 14" x 12" rectangle. Brush the dough with 1/2 of the melted butter. Mix the filling together and sprinkle half of it on the dough. Roll the dough up like a jelly roll and place it on a greased baking sheet. Shape the roll into a ring and pinch the seam together. Cut at 1" intervals with scissors. Twist each cut to show the filling.

2ND RISING
Set the baking sheet in a warm, draft-free spot and allow to rise until double: 30 minutes. If the dough rises in too warm a spot the ring will lose its shape.

EGG WASH
Just before baking brush the dough with egg wash (page 21).

BAKE
Bake at **350°F** in oven for **30-35 minutes.** Cover the bread with aluminum foil if the fruit starts to darken too quickly. Cool immediately after baking on a wire rack.

GLAZE
Drizzle with Icing Sugar Glaze (page 22) while still warm. Decorate with glacé cherries.

Glossary

BREAD BOWL

A very large bowl that will easily hold 14 cups. Ceramic and plastic bowls are recommended over steel bowls because they retain the heat better. A heavier bowl is easier to work with.

BREAD PANS

Remember to use the correct pan size or you will be disappointed with the bread's appearance.

8x4x3 inch sandwich loaf pans - the pans normally used in this book. Two will hold a recipe calling for 6½-8½ cups flour.

9x5x3 inch sandwich loaf pans - two will hold a recipe calling for 9-11 cups flour.

Cookie sheets or baking sheets - for free-form loaves. Use good quality sheets so that the bottom of the bread will not burn.

Glass pans - reduce the baking temperature by 50°F. If not the sides of the loaf will become very crusty and may burn.

Use dark, seasoned pans, not shiny new pans, so that the sides will brown during baking.

See sandwich loaves.

CARBON DIOXIDE

Yeast feeds on the sugar. The result of this chemical reaction is carbon dioxide (yeast + sugar yields carbon dioxide). Molasses, honey, brown sugar and potato starch are also good yeast food.

When the yeast gets trapped in the gluten mesh it feeds on the sugar, giving off carbon dioxide; then, as the carbon dioxide expands, so does the gluten meshwork, making the bread rise.

Two risings mature the carbon dioxide and gluten, thus making a nicer finished product.

COFFEE CAKE

Rich breads made with large quantities of fats, milk and eggs. To enhance their appearance they are brushed with egg wash before baking and glazed with icing sugar glaze after baking.

CORNMEAL

In this book, cornmeal is only used to prevent free-form loaves from sticking to the baking sheet. Sprinkle cornmeal only where the dough is to be set or it will burn during baking. Cornmeal is also used as an ingredient for such breads as Anadama.

DOUBLING A RECIPE

When doubling a bread recipe, only increase the salt and yeast by 1/2. For example, to double a recipe that calls for 1 tbsp. yeast and 2 tsp. salt, use 1½ tbsp. yeast and 3 tsp. salt (otherwise the salt and yeast concentration will be too high).

DRY MEASURE

Measuring cups that are full to the very top of the cup. Flour, sugar, whole grains, etc are accurately measured in a dry measure because the ingredient is levelled off at the top of the cup with a knife. (You cannot do this with a wet measure because it has extra space at the top of the cup to avoid spilling.) Do not shake the cup during measuring. See wet measure.

EGGS

The "magic" ingredient. Eggs add extra nutrition and richness to the bread. They will also make the bread yellow if used in large quantity. A bread made with eggs will have a greater than normal oven spring -thus the magic.

FATS

Shortening, oil, margarine, butter, lard, etc.
1) Flavour - margarine and butter make the bread rich tasting.
2) Fats act as a preservative. If the recipe does not contain a fat you must eat the bread on the same day that it is baked.
3) Fats also lubricate the gluten strands to make them stretch more easily.

FIRST RISING

This is the maturing process for gluten and yeast. A white bread which is baked after only one rising will be coarse-grained. Extra risings (2-3) improve the grain of the bread but too many risings (5 or more) will damage the gluten. First rising is always done in a clean, well greased bread bowl. See fool-proof-proofing, page 13.

FLOUR

Hard unbleached wheat flour is the best for making bread, it is chemical free and high in protein. This protein which turns into gluten during kneading, is one of the factors that make bread rise.

Rye flour is a nutritious flour but does not contain proteins that form gluten. As a result it should be mixed with wheat flour if you want the bread to rise. The same applies to CORN FLOUR, SOYA FLOUR, BARLEY FLOUR, etc.

FOOL-PROOF-PROOFING

Using the oven to allow bread to rise. Because the oven is the perfect draft-free spot for proofing, breadmaking is more predictable: first rising takes 1½-2 hours; second rising takes 30-45 minutes. To fool-proof-proof, boil 2 cups of water in a saucepan. Place the pan on the bottom rack of your oven. Place the dough on the rack directly above the water and do not cover the bread with a tea towel. Turn the lightbulb on in your oven and allow the dough to double. If you don't have a light in your oven reheat the water if the oven cools off. Don't place the dough too close to the lightbulb or it will bake. Remember, cover the bread with a tea towel only if you are not letting it rise in the oven.

FREE-FORM LOAVES

Round or oblong loaves that rise on a cookie sheet instead of in a loaf pan. Because the sides of the loaf are not supported, the dough must be stiff, otherwise the dough will spread out sideways instead of rising upward. Free-form loaves must be slashed on top just before baking to make room for oven spring. If the top is not slashed the base of the loaf will split during baking.

GLUTEN

There are proteins in wheat flour that react chemically when kneaded with water. These proteins are called gluten, and they form the framework of the bread by trapping the yeast and stretching with the resulting carbon dioxide. Only wheat flour has gluten and only hard wheat flour has enough of it to make bread. Rye, soy, corn and any other flour must be combined with wheat flour to make bread.

GRAIN (in the bread)

Bread quality is judged by the grain (texture) of the sliced loaf. A bread is either fine grained or coarse grained, the latter being the least desirable. If a bread has hardly any grain, it is called dense (which always happens when the bread doesn't rise).

GREASE THE BOWL

For the first rising grease your clean bread bowl. By placing the dough in the bowl and turning it to grease the top you are coating the dough with a fat that will prevent the top from drying out. Always use a fat that is solid in its normal state like margarine, butter, shortening or lard. Never use oil because, unlike a solid fat, oil penetrates into the dough making it stick to its container.

"GREEN" FLOUR

If you are lucky enough to live near a good flour mill you may be buying flour that is too young for making bread. Newly milled flour must mature for 6-8 weeks before it develops the qualities for making good bread.

KNEAD

The action used to develop the gluten in wheat flour. Kneading is a gentle, rhythmic, roll-push-turn motion that improves with practice. Always knead for 10 minutes when you are using a recipe which calls for 5-7 cups of flour. If you do not knead long enough the bread will be coarse and have an unpleasant "yeasty" taste.

KNIVES, BREAD

A serrated knife that catches the bread as it cuts, making it much easier to slice. Use an electric knife to slice hot bread.

MILK

Improves the protein content of bread. Makes the crust browner and the interior whiter. Do not use it to proof yeast.

Scalding stops milk from souring during the long, hot, first and second risings. To scald, pour the milk in a saucepan and heat it over medium heat until it starts to smoke and bubbles form around the edge of the pan. Cool to lukewarm before using. Skim milk powder is easy to use because it doesn't need to be scalded and is easy to store. Use it for all of your baking.

OVEN SPRING

During the first 10 minutes of baking the bread expands. This is due to the carbon dioxide gas trapped in the gluten meshwork. When gas is heated it expands, thus stretching the gluten meshwork and giving extra height to the bread. If the bread has over risen the oven spring will break the gluten meshwork and the bread will fall.

OVER RISING

If the bread looks light and airy and you know it has risen for too long it has over risen. This is only a problem with a dough that is ready to be baked. It may look nice before baking but during baking it will collapse. Keep an eye on timing: If necessary, punch it down, reshape it and set it to rise again. The third rising is faster.

POTATOES

Potatoes give the finished product a lovely fine textured grain that is different from any other main ingredient. Yeast feeds on potato starch so the dough does not require any other sugar except for taste. But, the dough will require more salt to control the growth of this over-fed yeast. The best potatoes to use are leftover mashed potatoes. Make potato bread on Monday from Sunday's leftover potatoes.

SALT
1) Controls the growth of yeast. Without salt your bread would be coarse and crumbly because the yeast would grow out of control.
2) Taste.
3) Dries the gluten strands out to make the dough feel smooth.

SANDWICH LOAVES
Any loaf that fits into a regular bread pan. These pans are normally 9x5x3 or 8x4x3 inch. Make sure that the amount of dough you are using is right for the pan. If the dough is from 6-8 cups of flour, use an 8x4x3 inch pan; if the dough is from 9-11 cups of flour, use a 9x5x3 inch pan. The dough for a sandwich loaf can be softer because the sides of the pan will support the dough.

SCALDING - see milk.

SECOND RISING
Takes place in the pan in which the dough is to be baked. It usually takes from 30-45 minutes using fool-proof-proofing. If the bread rises for too long it will fall during baking, so it is better to turn the dough out of the pan and reshape it. See fool-proof-proofing.

SKIM MILK POWDER - see milk.

SLASHING THE LOAVES
For free-form loaves. Using a very sharp knife or razor blade, make 3 or 4 deep diagonal cuts in the free-form loaf, just before baking. This helps to prevent the sides from splitting during oven spring.

SOFT DOUGH (Add flour slowly)
Sandwich loaves, dinner rolls, pizzas, chelsea buns, etc. can be made from soft doughs because the pans will support their sides as they rise. A soft dough produces a lighter textured product. To make a soft dough, pour 1 cup of flour into the bowl at a time and stir until smooth. The more you stir, the more the water is absorbed into the flour and the softer the dough. See Stiff Dough.

STIFF DOUGH (Add flour quickly)
Free-form loaves need stiff doughs so they will retain their shapes. To make a stiff dough, add the flour very quickly and barely stir after each addition. The more you stir, the more water is absorbed into the flour and the softer the dough will be. Add more flour if the dough is too soft and that will make a stiff dough as well. To judge if the dough is stiff, pinch a floured piece of it while it is still in your bread bowl, if it is dry and retains it shape, it is stiff. See Soft Dough.

SUGAR

1) Sugar is necessary to feed the yeast. It makes the yeast give off carbon dioxide gas which in turn makes bread rise.

2) Sugar is added for flavour. A coffee cake would not be the same without it.

3) Without sugar the crust of the bread will not brown. Notice this when you make Potato Bread or if you forget to put sugar in a recipe.

UNDER RISING

If you bake bread before it has doubled, it will split sideways when it bakes and the grain will be dense.

WATER AND WATER QUALITY

Water does not alter the flavour of bread, thus preserving the natural taste of the wheat. It is also the best liquid to proof your yeast in because it does not interfere with the chemical reaction. The water quality in certain towns and cities is not good for making bread. For example if the water is too soft the dough will be soft and sticky, and if the water is too hard the gluten will develop too much and the dough will not rise.

WET MEASURE

A cup with an extra half-inch above the final marking to avoid spilling the liquid being measured. These measures are not good for dry ingredients because the top cannot be levelled off. If you use a wet measure full to the top with dry ingredients you will have more than required in the recipe. See Dry Measure.

WHISK

An egg-shaped tool constructed with thin wires and usually a solid metal handle. Use one when you are making coffee cakes and other breads that incorporate a lot of ingredients during mixing. Stop using it after 2 cups of flour or you will never get all of the dough out of it.

YEAST

Yeast is a living plant. When it is kept in a cool spot like the refrigerator it remains dormant. Once it comes in contact with a warm liquid (usually water) it starts to expand and multiply, especially with the help of sugar. Sugar feeds the yeast and the result of the chemical reaction is carbon dioxide. Yeast will not grow if it is too cold and it will die if it is too hot (over 115°F).